Richard Glover

Leonidas

Vol. 2, sixth Edition

Richard Glover

Leonidas
Vol. 2, sixth Edition

ISBN/EAN: 9783744715508

Printed in Europe, USA, Canada, Australia, Japan

Cover: Foto ©Thomas Meinert / pixelio.de

More available books at **www.hansebooks.com**

LEONIDAS,

A POEM,

BY
RICHARD GLOVER.

ADORNED WITH PLATES.

VOL. II.

THE SIXTH EDITION.

LONDON:
Printed by T. Bensley;
FOR F. J. DU ROVERAY, GREAT ST. HELENS;
AND SOLD BY T. BOOSEY, OLD BROAD STREET;
AND J. WRIGHT, PICCADILLY.

1798.

LEONIDAS.

BOOK VII.

VOL. II.

THE ARGUMENT.

Megistias delivers Melissa's message to Leonidas. Medon, her brother, conducts him to the Temple. She furnishes Leonidas with the means of executing a design he had premeditated to annoy the enemy. They are joined by a body of mariners under the command of Æschylus, a celebrated poet and warrior among the Athenians. Leonidas takes the necessary measures; and, observing, from a summit of Oeta, the motions of the Persian army, expects another attack: this is renewed with great violence by Hyperanthes, Abrocomes, and the principal Persian leaders, at the head of some chosen troops.

LEONIDAS.

BOOK VII.

M<small>EGISTIAS</small>, urging to unwonted speed
His aged steps, by Dithyrambus charg'd
With sage Melissa's words, had now rejoin'd
The king of Lacedæmon. At his side
Was Maron posted, watchful to receive
His high injunctions. In the rear they stood
Behind two thousand Locrians, deep array'd
By warlike Medon, from Oïleus sprung.
Leonidas to them his anxious mind
Was thus disclosing—' Medon, Maron, hear.
From this low rampart my exploring eye
But half commands the action, yet hath mark'd
Enough for caution. Yon barbarian camp,
Immense, exhaustless, deluging the ground
With myriads, still o'erflowing, may consume,
By endless numbers and unceasing toil,

The Grecian strength. Not marble is our flesh,
Nor adamant our sinews. Silvan pow'rs,
Who dwell on Oeta, your superior aid
We must solicit. Your stupendous cliffs,
In those loose rocks and branchless trunks, contain
More fell annoyance than the arm of man.'

He ended; when Megistias—' Virtuous king,
Melissa, priestess of the tuneful nine,
By their behests, invites thy honour'd feet
To her chaste dwelling, seated on that hill.
To conference of high import she calls
Thee, first of Grecians.' Medon interpos'd—

' She is my sister. Justice rules her ways
With piety and wisdom. To her voice
The nations round give ear. The muses breathe
Their inspiration through her spotless soul,
Which borders on divinity. She calls
On thee. O, truly styl'd the first of Greeks,
Regard her call! Yon cliff's projecting head
To thy discernment will afford a scope
More full, more certain; thence thy skilful eye

Will best direct the fight.' Melissa's sire
Was ever present to the king in thought,
Who thus to Medon—' Lead, Oïleus' son:
Before the daughter of Oïleus place
My willing feet.' They hasten to the cave.
Megistias, Maron, follow. Through the rock
Leonidas, ascending to the fane,
Rose, like the god of morning from the cell
Of night, when, shedding cheerfulness and day
On hill and vale, emblaz'd with dewy gems,
He gladdens nature. Lacedæmon's king,
Majestically graceful and serene,
Dispels the rigour in that solemn seat
Of holy sequestration. On the face
Of pensive-ey'd religion rapture glows,
In admiration of the godlike man.
Advanc'd Melissa. He her proffer'd hand,
In hue, in purity, like snow, receiv'd.
A heav'n-illumin'd dignity of look
On him she fix'd. Rever'd by all, she spake—

' Hail, chief of men, selected by the gods
For purer fame than Hercules acquir'd!

This hour allows no pause.' She leads the king,
With Medon, Maron, and Megistias, down
A slope, declining to the mossy verge
Which terminates the mountain. While they pass
She thus proceeds—' These marble masses view,
Which lie dispers'd around you. They were hewn
From yonder quarry. Note those pond'rous beams,
The silvan offspring of that hill. With these,
At my request, th' Amphictyons, from their seat
Of gen'ral council, piously decreed
To raise a dome, the ornament of Greece.
Observe those wither'd firs, those mould'ring oaks,
Down that declivity, half-rooted, bent,
Inviting human force. Then look below.
There lies Thermopylæ.' ' I see,' exclaims
The high-conceiving hero. ' I recall
Thy father's words and forecast. He presag'd
I should not find his daughter's counsel vain.
He, to accomplish what thy wisdom plans,
Hath amplest means supply'd. Go, Medon, bring
The thousand peasants, from th' Oïlean vale
Detach'd. Their leader, Melibœus, bring.
Fly, Maron. Ev'ry instrument provide

To fell the trees, to drag the massy beams,
To lift the broad-hewn fragments.' ' Are not these
For sacred use reserv'd?' Megistias said.
' Can these be wielded by the hand of Mars
Without pollution?' In a solemn tone
The priestess answer'd—' Rev'rend man, who bear'st
Pontific wreaths, and thou, great captain, hear.
Forbear to think that my unprompted mind,
Calm and sequester'd in religion's peace,
Could have devis'd a stratagem of war;
Or, unpermitted, could resign to Mars
These rich materials, gather'd to restore,
In strength and splendour, yon decrepit walls,
And that time-shaken roof. Rejecting sleep,
Last night I lay, contriving swift revenge
On these Barbarians, whose career profane
O'erturns the Grecian temples, and devotes
Their holy bow'rs to flames. I left my couch
Long ere the sun his orient gates unbarr'd.
Beneath yon beach my pensive head reclin'd.
The rivulets, the fountains, warbling round,
Attracted slumber. In a dream I saw
Calliopé. Her sisters, all with harps,

Were rang'd around her; as their Parian forms
Shew in the temple. " Dost thou sleep?" she said;
" Melissa, dost thou sleep? The barb'rous host
Approaches Greece. The first of Grecians comes,
By death to vanquish. Priestess, let him hurl
These marble heaps, these consecrated beams,
Our fane itself, to crush the impious ranks.
The hero summon to our sacred hill.
Reveal the promis'd succour. All is due
To liberty against a tyrant's pride."
She struck her shell. In concert full reply'd
The sister lyres. Leonidas they sung,
In ev'ry note and dialect yet known,
In measures new, in language yet to come.'

She finish'd. Then Megistias—' Dear to heav'n,
By nations honour'd, and, in tow'ring thought,
O'er either sex pre-eminent, thy words
To me, a soldier and a priest, suffice.
I hesitate no longer.' But the king,
Wrapt in ecstatic contemplation, stood,
Revolving deep an answer, which might suit
His dignity and hers. At length he spake—

' Not Lacedæmon's whole collected state
Of senate, people, ephori, and kings;
Not the Amphictyons, whose convention holds
The universal majesty of Greece,
E'er drew such rev'rence as thy single form,
O all-surpassing woman, worthy child
Of time-renown'd Oïleus! In thy voice
I hear the goddess Liberty. I see,
In thy sublimity of look and port,
That daughter bright of Eleutherian Jove.
Me thou hast prais'd. My conscious spirit feels
That not to triumph in thy virtuous praise
Were want of virtue. Yet, illustrious dame,
Were I assur'd that oracles delude;
That, unavailing, I should spill my blood;
That all the Muses of subjected Greece
Hereafter would be silent, and my name
Be ne'er transmitted to recording time;
There is in virtue, for her sake alone,
What should uphold my resolution firm.
My country's laws I never would survive.'

Mov'd at his words, reflecting on his fate,

She had relax'd her dignity of mind,
Had sunk in sadness; but her brother's helm
Before her beams. Relumining her night,
He through the cave, like Hesperus, ascends,
Th' Oïlean hinds conducting, to achieve
The enterprise she counsels. Now her ear
Is pierc'd by notes, shrill sounding from the vault.
Upstarts a diff'rent band, alert and light,
Athenian sailors. Long and sep'rate files
Of lusty shoulders, eas'd by union, bear
Thick, well-compacted cables, wont to heave
The restiff anchor. To a naval pipe,
As if one soul invigorated all,
And all compos'd one body, they had trod
In equal paces, mazy, yet unbroke,
Throughout their passage. So the spinal strength
Of some portentous serpent, whom the heats
Of Libya breed, indissolubly knit,
But flexible, across the sandy plain,
Or up the mountain, draws his spotted length,.
Or where a winding excavation leads
Through rocks abrupt and wild. Of stature large,
In arms, which shew'd simplicity of strength,

No decoration of redundant art,
With sable horse-hair floating down his back,
A warrior moves behind. Compos'd in gait,
Austerely grave and thoughtful, on his shield
The democratic majesty he bore
Of Athens. Carv'd in emblematic brass,
Her image stood, with Pallas by her side,
And trampled under each victorious foot
A regal crown, one Persian, one usurpt
By her own tyrants, on the well-fought plain
Of Marathon confounded. He commands
These future guardians of their country's weal,
Of gen'ral Greece the bulwarks. Their high deeds
From Artemisium, from th' empurpled shores
Of Salamis, renown shall echo wide;
Shall tell posterity, in latest times,
That naval fortitude controls the world.
Swift Maron, following, brings a vig'rous band
Of Helots. Ev'ry instrument they wield
To delve, to hew, to heave; and, active, last
Bounds Melibœus, vigilant to urge
The tardy forward. To Laconia's king
Advanc'd th' Athenian leader, and began—

' Thou godlike ruler of Eurotas, hail!
Thee by my voice Themistocles salutes,
The admiral of Athens. I conduct,
By public choice, the squadron of my tribe,
And Æschylus am call'd. Our chief hath giv'n
Three days to glory on Eubœa's coast,
Whose promontories almost rise to meet
Thy ken from Oeta's cliffs. This morning saw
The worsted foe, from Artemisium driv'n,
Leave their disabled ships, and floating wrecks,
For Grecian trophies. When the fight was clos'd
I was detach'd to bring th' auspicious news,
To bid thee welcome. Fortunate, my keel
Hath swiftly borne me. Joyful I concur
In thy attempt. Appris'd by yonder chiefs,
Who met me landing, instant from the ships
A thousand gallant mariners I drew,
Who till the setting sun shall lend their toil.'

' Themistocles and thou accept my heart,'
Leonidas reply'd, and closely strain'd
The brave, the learn'd Athenian to his breast.
' To envy is ignoble; to admire

Th' activity of Athens will become
A king of Sparta, who, like thee, condemn'd
His country's sloth. But Sparta now is arm'd.
Thou shalt commend. Behold me, station'd here
To watch the wild vicissitudes of war,
Direct the course of slaughter. To this post
By that superior woman I was call'd.
By long protracted fight lest fainting Greece
Should yield, outnumber'd, my enlighten'd soul
Through her, whom heav'n enlightens, hath devis'd
To whelm the num'rous, persevering foe
In hideous death, and signalize the day
With horrors new to war. The Muses prompt
The bright achievement. Lo! from Athens smiles
Minerva too. Her swift, auspicious aid
In thee we find, and these, an ancient race,
By her and Neptune cherish'd.' Straight he meets
The gallant train; majestic, with his arms
Outstretch'd, in this applauding strain he spake—

' O lib'ral people, earliest arm'd, to shield
Not your own Athens more than gen'ral Greece,
You best deserve her gratitude. Her praise
Will rank you foremost on the rolls of fame.'

They hear, they gaze, revering, and rever'd.
Fresh numbers muster, rushing from the hills,
The thickets round.   Melissa, pointing, spake—

'I am their leader.   Natives of the hills
Are these, the rural worshippers of Pan,
Who breathes an ardour through their humble minds
To join you warriors.   Vassals these, not mine,
But of the Muses, and their hallow'd laws,
Administer'd by me.   Their patient hands
Make culture smile, where nature seems to chide;
Nor wanting my instructions, or my pray'rs,
Fertility they scatter, by their toil,
Around this aged temple's wild domain.
Is Melibœus here? Thou fence secure ..
To old Oïleus from the cares of time,
Thrice art thou welcome! Useful, wise, belov'd,
Where'er thou sojournest, on Oeta known,
As oft the bounty of a father's love
Thou on Melissa's solitude dost pour,
Be thou director of these mountain hinds!'

Th' important labour, to inspiring airs,

From flutes and harps, in symphony, with hymns
Of holy virgins, ardent all perform,
In bands divided under diff'rent chiefs.
Huge timbers, blocks of marble, to remove
They first attempted; then assembled stones,
Loose in their beds, and wither'd trunks, uptorn
By tempests; next dismember'd from the rock
Broad, rugged fragments; from the mountains hew'd
Their venerable firs and aged oaks,
Which, of their branches by the lightning bar'd,
Presented still against the blasting flame
Their hoary pride, unshaken. These the Greeks,
But chief th' Athenian mariners, to force
Uniting skill with massy leavers heave,
With strong-knit cables drag; till, now dispos'd
Where great Leonidas appoints, the piles
Nod o'er the Straits. This new and sudden scene
Might lift imagination to belief
That Orpheus and Amphion from their beds
Of ever-blooming asphodel had heard
The Muses call; had brought their fabled harps,
At whose mellifluent charm once more the trees
Had burst their fibrous bands, and marbles leap'd

In rapid motion from the quarry's womb,
That day to follow harmony, in aid
Of gen'rous valour. Fancy might discern
Cerulean Thetis, from her coral grot
Emerging, seated on her pearly car,
With Nereids, floating on the surge below,
To view, in wonder, from the Malian bay
The attic sons of Neptune, who forsook
Their wooden walls to range th' Oetæan crags,
To rend the forests, and disjoin the rocks.

Meantime a hundred sheep are slain. Their limbs
From burning piles fume grateful. Bounty spreads
A decent board. Simplicity attends.
Then spake the priestess—' Long-enduring chiefs,
Your efforts, now accomplish'd, may admit
Refection, due to this hard-labour'd train,
Due to yourselves.' Her hospitable smile
Wins her well-chosen guests, Laconia's king,
Her brother, Maron, Æschylus divine,
With Acarnania's priest. Her first commands
To Melibœus, sedulous and blithe,
Distribute plenty through the toiling crowd.

Then, screen'd beneath close umbrage of an oak,
Each care-divested chief the banquet shares.

    Cool breezes, whisp'ring, flutter in the leaves,
Whose verdure, pendent in an arch, repel
The west'ring sun's hot glare. Favonius bland
His breath impregnates with exhaling sweets
From flow'ry beds, whose scented clusters deck
The gleaming pool in view. Fast by a brook,
In limpid lampses, over native steps
Attunes his cadence to sonorous strings,
And liquid accents of Melissa's maids.
The floating air in melody respires.
A rapture mingles in the calm repast,
Uprises Æschylus. A goblet full
He grasps—' To those divinities who dwell
In yonder temple, this libation first;
To thee, benignant hostess, next I pour;
Then to thy fame, Leonidas.' He said.
His breast, with growing heat distended, prompts
His eager hand, to whose expressive sign
One of the virgins cedes her sacred lyre.
Their choral song complacency restrains.

The soul of music, bursting from his touch,
At once gives birth to sentiment sublime.

' O Hercules and Perseus,' he began,
' Star-spangled twins of Leda, and the rest
Of Jove's immediate seed, your splendid acts
Mankind protected while the race was rude;
While o'er the earth's unciviliz'd extent
The savage monster and the ruffian sway'd,
More savage still. No policy, nor laws,
Had fram'd societies. By single strength
A single ruffian or a monster fell.
The legislator rose. Three lights in Greece,
Lycurgus, Solon, and Zaleucus, blaz'd.
Then, substituting wisdom, Jove, profuse
Of his own blood no longer, gave us more
In discipline and manners, which can form
A hero like Leonidas, than all
The god-begotten progeny before.
The pupils next of Solon claim the muse.
Sound your hoarse conchs, ye Tritons. You beheld
The Atlantēan shape of slaughter wade
Through your astonish'd deeps, his purple arm

Uplifting high before th' Athenian line.
You saw bright conquest, riding on the gale
Which swell'd their sails; saw terror at their helms,
To guide their brazen beaks on Asia's pride.
Her adamantine grapple from their decks
Fate threw, and ruin on the hostile fleet
Inextricably fasten'd. Sound, ye nymphs
Of Oeta's mountains, of her woods and streams,
Who hourly witness to Melissa's worth,
Ye Oreads, Dryads, Naiads, sound her praise!
Proclaim Zaleucus by his daughter grac'd,
Like Solon and Lycurgus by their sons.'

Laconia's hero, and the priestess, bow'd
Their foreheads grateful to the bard sublime.
She, rising, takes the word—' More sweet thy lyre
To friendship's ear than terrible to foes
Thy spear in battle, though the keenest point
Which ever pierc'd Barbarians. Close we here
The song and banquet. Hark! a distant din
From Asia's camp requires immediate care!'

She leads. Along the rocky verge they pass.

In calm delight, Leonidas surveys
All in the order which he last assign'd,
As o'er Thermopylæ beneath he cast
A wary look. The mountain's furthest crag
Now reach'd, Melissa to the king began—

' Observe that space below, dispers'd in dales,
In hollows, winding through dissever'd rocks.
The slender outlet, screen'd by yonder shrubs,
Leads to the pass. There stately, to my view
The martial queen of Caria, yester sun
Descending shew'd. Her loudly I reprov'd.
But she, devoted to the Persian king,
In ambush there preserv'd his flying host.
She last retreated; but, retreating, prov'd
Her valour equal to a better cause.
Again I see the heroine approach.'

Megistias then—' I see a pow'rful arm,
Sustaining firm the large, emblazon'd shield,
Which, fashion'd first in Caria, we have learn'd
To imitate in Greece. Sublime, her port
Bespeaks a mighty spirit. Priestess, look.

An act of piety she now performs,
Directing those, perhaps her Carian band,
To bear dead brethren from the bloody field.
Among the horsemen an exalted form,
Like Demaratus, strikes my searching eye.
To me, recalling his transcendent rank
In Sparta once, he seems a languid sun,
Which dimly sinks in exhalations dark,
Enveloping his radiance.' While he spake,
Intent on martial duty, Medon views
The dang'rous thicket; Lacedæmon's chief,
Around the region his consid'rate eye
Extending, marks each movement of the foe.

Th' imperial Persian, from his lofty car,
Had, in the morning's early conflict, seen
His vanquish'd army pouring from the straits
Back to their tents, and o'er his camp dispers'd
In consternation; as a river bursts
Impetuous from his fountain, then, enlarg'd,
Spreads a dead surface o'er some level marsh.
Th' astonish'd king thrice started from his seat;
Shame, fear, and indignation rent his breast;

As ruin irresistible were near
To overwhelm his millions. ' Haste!' he call'd
To Hyperanthes, ' haste, and meet the Greeks.
Their daring rage, their insolence, repel.
From such dishonour vindicate our name.'

 His royal brother through th' extensive camp
Obedient mov'd. Deliberate and brave,
Each active prince, from ev'ry tent remote,
The hardiest troops, he summon'd. Caria's queen,
To Hyperanthes bound by firm esteem
Of worth, unrivall'd in the Persian court,
In solemn pace was now returning slow
Before a band, transporting from the field
Their slain companions to the sandy beach.

 She stopt, and thus address'd him. ' Learn, O prince,
From one whose wishes on thy merit wait,
The only means to bind thy gallant brow
In fairest wreaths. To break the Grecian line
In vain ye struggle, unarray'd and lax,
Depriv'd of union. Try to form one band
In order'd ranks, and emulate the foe.

.

Nor to secure a thicket next the pass
Forget. Selected numbers station there.
Farewell, young hero! May thy fortune prove
Unlike to mine. Had Asia's millions spar'd
One myriad to sustain me, none had seen
Me quit the dang'rous contest. But the head
Of base Argestes on some future day
Shall feel my treasur'd vengeance. From the fleet
I only stay till burial rites are paid
To these dead Carians. On this fatal strand
May Artemisia's grief appease your ghosts,
My faithful subjects, sacrific'd in vain.'

The hero grateful and respectful heard
What soon his warmth neglected, at the sight
Of spears which flam'd innumerable round.
Beyond the rest in lustre was a band,
The satellites of Xerxes. They forsook
Their constant orbit round th' imperial throne
At this dread crisis. To a myriad fix'd,
From their unchanging number they deriv'd
The title of immortals. Light their spears;
Set in pomegranates of refulgent gold,

Or burnish'd silver, were the slender blades.
Magnificent and stately were the ranks.
The prince, commanding mute attention, spake—

'In two divisions part your number, chiefs.
One will I lead to onset. In my ranks
Abrocomes, Hydarnes, shall advance,
Pandates, Mindus, Intaphernes brave,
To wrest this short-liv'd victory from Greece.
Thou, Abradates, by Sosarmes join'd,
Orontes and Mazæus, keep the rest
From action. Future succour they must lend,
Should envious fate exhaust our num'rous files;
For, O pure Mithra, may thy radiant eye
Ne'er see us, yielding to ignoble flight,
The Persian name dishonour. May the acts
Of our renown'd progenitors, who, led
By Cyrus, gave one monarch to the east,
In us revive. O think, ye Persian lords,
What endless infamy will blast your names,
Should Greece, that narrow portion of the earth,
Your pow'r defy; when Babylon hath low'r'd
Her tow'ring crest; when Lydia's pride is quell'd

In Crœsus vanquish'd; when her empire lost
Ecbatana deplores! Ye chosen guard,
Your king's immortal bulwark, O reflect
What deeds from your superior swords he claims!
You share his largest bounty. To your faith,
Your constancy and prowess, he commits
His throne, his person, and this day his fame!'

    They wave their banners, blazing in the sun,
Who then three hours tow'rd Hesperus had driv'n
From his meridian height. Amid their shouts
The hoarse-resounding billows are not heard.
Of diff'rent nations, and in diff'rent garb,
Innumerous and vary'd, like the shells
By restless Thetis scatter'd on the beach
O'er which they trod, the multitude advanc'd,
Straight by Leonidas descry'd. The van
Abrocomes and Hyperanthes led,
Pandates, Mindus. Violent their march
Sweeps down the rocky, hollow-sounding pass.
So, where th' unequal globe in mountains swells,
A torrent rolls his thund'ring surge between
The steep-erected cliffs; tumultuous dash

The waters, bursting on the pointed crags;
The valley roars; the marble channel foams.
Th' undaunted Greeks immoveably withstand
The dire encounter. Soon th' impetuous shock
Of thousands and of myriads shakes the ground.
Stupendous scene of terror! Under hills,
Whose sides half-arching o'er the hosts project,
The unabating fortitude of Greece
Maintains her line; th' untrain'd Barbarians charge
In savage fury. With inverted trunks,
Or bent obliquely from the shagged ridge,
The silvan horrors overshade the fight.
The clanging trump, the crash of mingled spears,
The groan of death, and war's discordant shouts,
Alarm the echoes in their neighb'ring caves;
Woods, cliffs, and shores, return the dreadful sound.

LEONIDAS.

BOOK VIII.

THE ARGUMENT.

Hyperanthes, discontinuing the fight while he waits for reinforcements, Teribazus, a Persian remarkable for his merit and learning, and highly beloved by Hyperanthes, but unhappy in his passion for Ariana, a daughter of Darius, advances from the rest of the army to the rescue of a friend in distress, who lay wounded on the field of battle. Teribazus is attacked by Diophantüs, the Mantinean, whom he overcomes; then, engaging with Dithyrambus, is himself slain. Hyperanthes hastens to his succour. A general battle ensues, where Diomedon distinguishes his valour. Hyperanthes and Abrocomes, partly by their own efforts, and partly by the perfidy of the Thebans, who desert the line, being on the point of forcing the Grecians, are repulsed by the Lacedæmonians. Hyperanthes composes a select body out of the Persian standing forces, and, making an improvement in their discipline, renews the attack; upon which Leonidas changes the disposition of his army. Hyperanthes and the ablest Persian generals are driven out of the field, and several thousands of the Barbarians, circumvented in the pass, are entirely destroyed.

LEONIDAS.

BOOK VIII.

AMID the van of Persia was a youth,
Nam'd Teribazus; not for golden stores;
Not for wide pastures, travers'd o'er by herds,
By fleece abounding sheep, or gen'rous steeds,
Nor yet for pow'r, nor splendid honours, fam'd.
Rich was his mind in ev'ry art divine;
Through ev'ry path of science had he walk'd,
The votary of wisdom.   In the years
When tender down invests the ruddy cheek,
He with the Magi turn'd the hallow'd page
Of Zoroastres.   Then his tow'ring thoughts
High on the plumes of contemplation soar'd.
He, from the lofty Babylonian fane,
With learn'd Chaldæans trac'd the heav'nly sphere;
There number'd o'er the vivid fires which gleam

On night's bespangled bosom. Nor unheard
Were Indian sages from sequester'd bow'rs,
While on the banks of Ganges they disclos'd
The pow'rs of nature, whether in the woods,
The fruitful glebe, or flow'r, the healing plant,
The limpid waters, or the ambient air,
Or in the purer element of fire.
The realm of old Sesostris next he view'd,
Mysterious Egypt, with her hidden rites
Of Isis and Osiris. Last he sought
Th' Ionian Greeks, from Athens sprung; nor pass'd
Miletus by, which once in rapture heard
The tongue of Thales; nor Priene's walls,
Where wisdom dwelt with Bias; nor the seat
Of Pittacus, rever'd on Lesbian shores.

Th' enlighten'd youth to Susa now return'd,
Place of his birth. His merit soon was dear
To Hyperanthes. It was now the time
That discontent and murmur on the banks
Of Nile were loud and threat'ning. Chembes there
The only faithful stood, a potent lord,
Whom Xerxes held by promis'd nuptial ties

With his own blood. To this Ægyptian prince
Bright Ariana was the destin'd spouse,
From the same bed with Hyperanthes born.
Among her guards was Teribazus nam'd
By that fond brother, tender of her weal.

Th' Ægyptian boundaries they gain. They hear
Of insurrection, of the Pharian tribes
In arms, and Chembes in the tumult slain.
They pitch their tents, at midnight are assail'd,
Surpris'd, their leaders massacred, the slaves
Of Ariana captives borne away,
Her own pavilion forc'd, her person seiz'd
By ruffian hands; when timely, to redeem
Her and th' invaded camp from further spoil,
Flies Teribazus with a rally'd band,
Swift on her chariot seats the royal fair,
Nor waits the dawn. Of all her menial train
None but three female slaves are left. Her guide,
Her comforter and guardian, fate provides
In him, distinguish'd by his worth alone,
No prince, nor satrap, now the single chief
Of her surviving guard. Of regal birth,

But with excelling graces in her soul,
Unlike an eastern princess, she inclines
To his consoling, his instructive, tongue
An humbled ear. Amid the converse sweet,
Her charms, her mind, her virtues, he explores,
Admiring. Soon is admiration chang'd
To love; nor loves he sooner than despairs.
From morn till ev'n her passing wheels he guards
Back to Euphrates. Often, as she mounts
Or quits the car, his arm her weight sustains
With trembling pleasure. His assiduous hand
From purest fountains wafts the living flood.
Nor seldom, by the fair one's soft command
Would he repose him, at her feet reclin'd;
While o'er his lips her lovely forehead bow'd,
Won by his grateful eloquence, which sooth'd
With sweet variety the tedious march,
Beguiling time. He too would then forget
His pains awhile, in raptures vain entranc'd;
Delusion all, and fleeting rays of joy,
Soon overcast by more intense despair.
Like wintry clouds, which, op'ning for a time,
Tinge their black folds with gleams of scatter'd light,

Then, swiftly closing, on the brow of morn
Condense their horrors, and in thickest gloom
The ruddy beauty veil. They now approach
The tow'r of Belus. Hyperanthes leads
Through Babylon an army to chastize
The crime of Ægypt. Teribazus here
Parts from his princess, marches bright in steel
Beneath his patron's banner, gathers palms
On conquer'd Nile. To Susa he returns,
To Ariana's residence, and bears
Deep in his heart th' immedicable wound.
But unreveal'd and silent was his pain;
Nor yet in solitary shades he roam'd,
Nor shun'd resort: but o'er his sorrows cast
A sickly dawn of gladness, and in smiles
Conceal'd his anguish; while the secret flame
Rag'd in his bosom, and its peace consum'd,
His soul still brooding o'er these mournful thoughts—

' Can I, O Wisdom, find relief in thee,
Who dost approve my passion? From the snares
Of beauty only thou wouldst guard my heart.
But here thyself art charm'd; where softness, grace,

And ev'ry virtue, dignify desire.
Yet thus to love, despairing to possess,
Of all the torments, by relentless fate
On life inflicted, is the most severe.
Do I not feel thy warnings in my breast,
That flight alone can save me? I will go
Back to the learn'd Chaldæans, on the banks
Of Ganges seek the sages; where to heav'n
With thee my elevated soul shall tow'r.
O wretched Teribazus! all conspires
Against thy peace. Our mighty lord prepares
To overwhelm the Grecians. Ev'ry youth
Is call'd to war; and I, who lately pois'd
With no inglorious arm the soldier's lance,
Who near the side of Hyperanthes fought,
Must join the throng. How therefore can I fly
From Ariana, who with Asia's queens
The splendid camp of Xerxes must adorn?
Then be it so. Again I will adore
Her gentle virtues. Her delightful voice,
Her gracious sweetness, shall again diffuse
Resistless magic through my ravish'd heart;
Till passion, thus with double rage inflam'd,

Swells to distraction in my tortur'd breast;
Then—but in vain through darkness do I search
My fate—Despair and fortune be my guides!'

    The day arriv'd when Xerxes first advanc'd
His arms from Susa's gates. The Persian dames,
So were accustom'd all the eastern fair,
In sumptuous cars accompany'd his march;
A beauteous train, by Ariana grac'd.
Her Teribazus follows, on her wheels
Attends and pines. Such woes oppress the youth,
Oppress, but not enervate. From the van
He in this second conflict had withstood
The threat'ning frown of adamantine Mars;
He singly, while his bravest friends recoil'd.
His manly temples no tiara bound.
The slender lance of Asia he disdain'd,
And her light target. Eminent he tow'r'd
In Grecian arms the wonder of his foes;
Among th' Ionians were his strenuous limbs
Train'd in the gymnic school. A fulgent casque
Enclos'd his head. Before his face and chest,
Down to the knees, an ample shield was spread.

A pond'rous spear he shook. The well-aim'd point
Sent two Phliasians to the realms of death,
With four Tegæans; whose indignant chief,
Brave Hegesander, vengeance breath'd in vain,
With streaming wounds repuls'd. Thus far, unmatch'd,
His arm prevail'd; when Hyperanthes call'd
From fight his fainting legions. Now each band .
Their languid courage reinforc'd by rest.
Meantime with Teribazus thus conferr'd
Th' applauding prince—' Thou much deserving youth,
Had twenty warriors in the dang'rous van
Like thee maintain'd the onset, Greece had wept
Her prostrate ranks. The weary'd fight awhile
I now relax, till Abradates strong,
Orontes and Mazæus, are advanc'd.
Then to the conflict will I give no pause.
If not by prowess, yet by endless toil
Successive numbers shall exhaust the foe.'

He said. Immers'd in sadness, scarce reply'd,
But to himself complain'd, the am'rous youth.

' Still do I languish, mourning o'er the fame

My arm acquires. Tormented heart! thou seat
Of constant sorrow, what deceitful smiles
Yet canst thou borrow from unreal hope
To flatter life? At Ariana's feet
What if with supplicating knees I bow,
Implore her pity, and reveal my love.
Wretch! canst thou climb to yon effulgent orb,
And share the splendours which irradiate heav'n?
Dost thou aspire to that exalted maid,
Great Xerxes' sister, rivalling the claim
Of Asia's proudest potentates and kings?
Unless within her bosom I inspir'd
A passion fervent as my own, nay more,
Such as, dispelling ev'ry virgin fear,
Might, unrestrain'd, disclose its fond desire,
My love is hopeless; and her willing hand,
Should she bestow it, draws from Asia's lord
On both perdition.' By despair benumb'd,
His limbs their action lose. A wish for death
O'ercasts and chills his soul. When sudden cries
From Ariamnes rouse his drooping pow'rs.
Alike in manners, they, of equal age,
Were friends, and partners in the glorious toil

Of war.   Together they victorious chas'd
The bleeding sons of Nile, when Ægypt's pride
Before the sword of Hyperanthes fell.
That lov'd companion Teribazus views
By all abandon'd, in his gore outstretch'd,
The victor's spoil.   His languid spirit starts;
He rushes ardent from the Persian line;
The wounded warrior in his strong embrace
He bears away.   By indignation stung,
Fierce from the Grecians, Diophantus sends
A loud defiance.   Teribazus leaves
His rescu'd friend.   His massy shield he rears;
High brandishing his formidable spear,
He turns intrepid on th' approaching foe.
Amazement follows.   On he strides, and shakes
The plumed honours of his shining crest.
Th' ill-fated Greek awaits th' unequal fight;
Pierc'd in the throat, with sounding arms he falls.
Through ev'ry file the Mantineans mourn.
Long on the slain the victor fix'd his sight
With these reflections—' By thy splendid arms
Thou art a Greek of no ignoble rank.
From thy ill fortune I perhaps derive

A more conspicuous lustre. What if heav'n
Should add new victims, such as thou, to grace
My undeserving hand? Who knows but she
Might smile upon my trophies? Oh! vain thought!
I see the pride of Asia's monarch swell
With vengeance, fatal to her beauteous head.
Disperse, ye phantom hopes! Too long, torn heart,
Hast thou with grief contended. Lo! I plant
My foot this moment on the verge of death,
By fame invited, by despair impell'd,
To pass th' irremeable bound. No more
Shall Teribazus backward turn his step,
But here conclude his doom. Then cease to heave,
Thou troubled bosom; ev'ry thought be calm
Now at th' approach of everlasting peace.'

He ended; when a mighty foe drew nigh,
Not less than Dithyrambus. Ere they join'd
The Persian warrior to the Greek began—

' Art thou th' unconquerable chief, who mow'd
Our battle down? That eagle on thy shield
Too well proclaims thee. To attempt thy force

I rashly purpos'd. That my single arm
Thou deign'st to meet, accept my thanks, and know
The thought of conquest less employs my soul
Than admiration of thy glorious deeds,
And that by thee I cannot fall disgrac'd.'

  He ceas'd. These words the Thespian youth return'd—
' Of all the praises from thy gen'rous mouth,
The only portion my desert may claim
Is this my bold adventure, to confront
Thee, yet unmatch'd. What Grecian hath not mark'd
Thy flaming steel? From Asia's boundless camp
Not one hath equall'd thy victorious might.
But whence thy armour of the Grecian form?
Whence thy tall spear, thy helmet? Whence the weight
Of that strong shield? Unlike thy eastern friends,
O if thou be'st some fugitive, who, lost
To liberty and virtue, art become
A tyrant's vile stipendiary, that arm,
That valour, thus triumphant, I deplore,
Which, after all their efforts and success,
Deserve no honour from the gods or men.'

Here Teribazus in a sigh rejoin'd—
' I am to Greece a stranger, am a wretch
To thee unknown, who courts this hour to die,
Yet not ignobly, but in death to raise
My name from darkness, while I end my woes.'

The Grecian then—' I view thee, and I mourn.
A dignity, which virtue only bears,
Firm resolution, seated on thy brow,
Though grief hath dimm'd thy drooping eye, demand
My veneration: and, whatever be
The malice of thy fortune, what the cares
Infesting thus thy quiet, they create
Within my breast the pity of a friend.
Why then, constraining my reluctant hand
To act against thee, will thy might support
Th' unjust ambition of malignant kings,
The foes to virtue, liberty, and peace?
Yet, free from rage or enmity, I lift
My adverse weapon. Victory I ask.
Thy life may fate for happier days reserve.'

This said, their beaming lances they protend,

Of hostile hate or fury both devoid,
As on the Isthmian or Olympic sands
For fame alone contending. Either host,
Pois'd on their arms, in silent wonder gaze.
The fight commences. Soon the Grecian spear,
Which, all the day in constant battle worn,
Unnumber'd shields and corselets had transfix'd,
Against the Persian buckler shiv'ring, breaks,
Its master's hand disarming. Then began
The sense of honour and the dread of shame,
To swell in Dithyrambus. Undismay'd,
He grappled with his foe, and instant seiz'd
His threat'ning spear, before th' uplifted arm
Could execute the meditated wound.
The weapon burst between their struggling grasp.
Their hold they loosen, bare their shining swords.
With equal swiftness to defend or charge,
Each active youth advances and recedes.
On ev'ry side they traverse. Now direct,
Obliquely now, the wheeling blades descend.
Still is the conflict dubious; when the Greek,
Dissembling, points his falchion to the ground,
His arm depressing, as o'ercome by toil;

While with his buckler cautious he repels
The blows, repeated by his active foe.
Greece trembles for her hero. Joy pervades
The ranks of Asia; Hyperanthes strides
Before the line, preparing to receive
His friend triumphant; while the wary Greek
Calm and defensive bears th' assault. At last,
As by th' incautious fury of his strokes,
The Persian swung his cov'ring shield aside;
The fatal moment Dithyrambus seiz'd.
Light darting forward, with his feet outstretch'd,
Between th' unguarded ribs he plung'd his steel.
Affection, grief, and terror, wing the speed
Of Hyperanthes. From his bleeding foe
The Greek retires, not distant, and awaits
The Persian prince. But he, with wat'ry cheeks,
In speechless anguish clasps his dying friend;
From whose cold lip, with interrupted phrase,
These accents break—' O dearest, best of men!
Ten thousand thoughts of gratitude and love
Are struggling in my heart—O'erpow'ring fate
Denies my voice the utt'rance—O my friend!
O Hyperanthes! Hear my tongue unfold

What, had I liv'd, thou never shouldst have known.
I lov'd thy sister! With despair I lov'd!
Soliciting this honourable doom,
Without regret, in Persia's sight and thine,
I fall.' Th' inexorable hand of fate
Weighs down his eyelids, and the gloom of death
His fleeting light eternally o'ershades.
Him on Choaspes o'er the blooming verge
A frantic mother shall bewail; shall strew
Her silver tresses in the crystal wave;
While all the shores re-echo to the name
Of Teribazus lost. Th' afflicted prince,
Contemplating in tears the pallid corse,
Vents in these words the bitterness of grief.

' Oh Teribazus! Oh my friend! whose loss
I will deplore for ever. Oh what pow'r,
By me, by thee offended, clos'd thy breast
To Hyperanthes, in distrust unkind!
She should, she must have lov'd thee! Now no more
Thy placid virtues, thy instructive tongue,
Shall drop their sweetness on my secret hours.

But in complaints doth friendship waste the time,
Which to immediate vengeance should be giv'n?'

He ended, rushing furious on the Greek;
Who, while his gallant enemy expir'd,
While Hyperanthes tenderly receiv'd
The last embraces of his gasping friend,
Stood nigh, reclin'd in sadness on his shield,
And in the pride of victory repin'd.
Unmark'd, his foe approach'd. But forward sprung
Diomedon. Before the Thespian youth
Aloft he rais'd his targe, and loudly thus—

' Hold thee, Barbarian, from a life more worth
Than thou and Xerxes, with his host of slaves.'

His words he seconds with his rapid lance.
Soon a tremendous conflict had ensu'd;
But Intaphernes, Mindus, and a crowd
Of Persian lords, advancing, fill the space
Betwixt th' encount'ring chiefs. In mutual wrath,
With fruitless efforts, they attempt the fight.
So rage two bulls along th' opposing banks

Of some deep flood, which parts the fruitful mead.
Defiance thunders from their angry mouths
In vain; in vain the furrow'd sod they rend;
Wide rolls the stream, and intercepts the war.

As, by malignant fortune, if a drop
Of moisture mingles with a burning mass
Of liquid metal, instant show'rs of death
On ev'ry side th' exploding fluid spreads;
So disappointment irritates the flame
Of fierce Platæa's chief, whose vengeance bursts
In wide destruction. Embas, Daucus, fall;
Arsæus, Ochus, Mendes, Artias, die;
And ten most hardy of th' immortal guard;
To shivers breaking on the Grecian shield
Their gold embellish'd weapons, raise a mound
O'er thy pale body, Oh in prime destroy'd,
Of Asia's garden once the fairest plant,
Fall'n Teribazus! Thy distracted friend
From this thy temporary tomb is dragg'd
By forceful zeal of satraps to the shore;
Where then the brave Abrocomes arrang'd
The succours new, by Abradates brought,

Orontes and Mazæus. Turning swift,
Abrocomes inform'd his brother thus—

' Strong reinforcement from th' immortal guard
Pandates bold to Intaphernes leads,
In charge to harass, by perpetual toil,
Those Grecians next the mountain. Thou unite
To me thy valour. Here the hostile ranks
Less stable seem. Our joint impression try;
Let all the weight of battle here impend.
Rouse, Hyperanthes! Give regret to winds.
Who hath not lost a friend this direful day?
Let not our private cares assist the Greeks,
Too strong already, or let sorrow act:
Mourn and revenge.' These animating words
Send Hyperanthes to the foremost line.
His vengeful ardour leads. The battle joins.

Who stemm'd this tide of onset? Who imbru'd
His shining spear the first in Persian blood?
Eupalamus. Artembares he slew,
With Derdas fierce, whom Caucasus had rear'd
On his tempestuous brow, the savage son;

Of violence and rapine. But their doom
Fires Hyperanthes, whose vindictive blade
Arrests the victor in his haughty course.
Beneath the strong Abrocomes o'erwhelm'd,
Melissus swells the number of the dead.
None could Mycenæ boast of prouder birth
Than young Melissus, who in silver mail
The line embellish'd. He in Cirrha's mead,
Where high Parnassus from his double top
O'ershades the Pythian games, the envy'd prize
Of fame obtain'd. Low sinks his laurell'd head
In death's cold night, and horrid gore deforms
The graceful hair. Impatient to revenge,
Aristobulus strides before the van.
A storm of fury darkens all his brow.
Around he rolls his gloomy eye. For death
Is Alyattes mark'd, of regal blood,
Deriv'd from Crœsus, once imperial lord
Of nations. Him the nymphs of Halys wept,
When, with delusive oracles beguil'd
By Delphi's god, he pass'd their fatal waves
A mighty empire to dissolve: nor knew
Th' ill-destin'd prince that envious fortune watch'd

That direful moment, from his hand to wrest
The sceptre of his fathers. In the shade
Of humble life his race on Tmolus' brow
Lay hid, till, rous'd to battle, on this field
Sinks Alyattes, and a royal breed
In him extinct for ever. Lycis dies,
For boist'rous war ill chosen. He was skill'd
To tune the lulling flute and melt the heart,
Or with his pipe's awak'ning strain allure
The lovely dames of Lydia to the dance.
They on the verdant level graceful mov'd
In vary'd measures; while the cooling breeze,
Beneath their swelling garments wanton'd o'er
Their snowy breasts, and smooth Cäyster's stream,
Soft-gliding, murmur'd by. The hostile blade
Draws forth his entrails. Prone he falls. Not long
The victor triumphs. From the prostrate corse
Of Lycis, while, insulting, he extracts
The reeking weapon, Hyperanthes' steel
Invades his knee, and cuts the sinewy cords.
The Mycenæans with uplifted shields,
Corinthians and Phliasians, close around
The wounded chieftain. In redoubled rage

The contest glows.   Abrocomes incites
Each noble Persian.   Each his voice obeys.
Here Abradates, there Mazæus, press,
Orontes and Hydarnes.   None retire
From toil or peril.   Urg'd on ev'ry side,
Mycenæ's band to fortune leave their chief.
Despairing, raging, destitute, he stands,
Propt on his spear.   His wound forbids retreat.
None, but his brother Eumenes, abides
The dire extremity.   His studded orb
Is held defensive.   On his arm the sword
Of Hyperanthes rapidly descends.
Down drops the buckler, and the sever'd hand
Resigns its hold.   The unprotected pair
By Asia's hero to the ground are swept;
As to a reaper crimson poppies low'r
Their heads, luxuriant on the yellow plain.
From both their breasts the vital currents flow,
And mix their streams.   Elate, the Persians pour
Their numbers, deep'ning on the foe, dismay'd.
The Greeks their station painfully maintain.
This Anaxander saw, whose faithless tongue
His colleague Leontiades bespake—

' The hour is come to serve our Persian friends.
Behold, the Greeks are press'd. Let Thebes retire,
A bloodless conquest yielding to the king.'

This said, he drew his Thebans from their post,
Not with unpunish'd treachery. The lance
Of Abradates gor'd their foul retreat;
Nor knew the Asian chief that Asia's friend
Before him bled. Meantime, as mighty Jove,
Or he more ancient on the throne of heav'n,
When from the womb of Chaos dark the world
Emerg'd to birth, where'er he view'd the jar
Of atoms yet discordant and unform'd,
Confusion thence with pow'rful voice dispell'd,
Till light and order universal reign'd;
So from the hill Leonidas survey'd
The various war. He saw the Theban rout;
That Corinth, Phlius, and Mycenæ, look'd
Affrighted backward. Instantly his charge
Is borne by Maron, whom obedience wings,
Precipitating down the sacred cave,
That Sparta's ranks, advancing, should repair
The disunited phalanx. Ere they move

Dieneces inspires them—' Fame, my friends,
Calls forth your valour in a signal hour.
For you this glorious crisis she reserv'd,
Laconia's splendour to assert. Young man,
Son of Megistias, follow.' He conducts
Th' experienc'd troop. They lock their shields, and, wedg'd
In dense arrangement, repossess the void
Left by the faithless Thebans, and repulse
Th' exulting Persians. When, with efforts vain,
These oft renew'd the contest, and recoil'd
As oft, confounded with diminish'd ranks,
Lo! Hyperanthes blush'd, repeating late
The words of Artemisia—' Learn, O chiefs,
The only means of glory and success.
Unlike the others, whom we newly chas'd,
These are a band selected from the Greeks,
Perhaps the Spartans, whom we often hear
By Demaratus prais'd. To break their line
In vain we struggle, unarray'd and lax,
Depriv'd of union. Do not we preside
O'er Asia's armies, and our courage boast,
Our martial art above the vulgar herd?

Let us, ye chiefs, attempt in order'd ranks
To form a troop, and emulate the foe.'

They wait not dubious. On the Malian shore
In gloomy depth a column soon is form'd
Of all the nobles; Abradates strong,
Orontes bold, Mazæus, and the might
Of brave Abrocomes, with each who bore
The highest honours, and excell'd in arms;
Themselves the lords of nations, who before
The throne of Xerxes tributary bow'd.
To these succeed a chosen number, drawn
From Asia's legions, vaunted most in fight;
Who from their king perpetual stipends share;
Who, station'd round the provinces, by force
His tyranny uphold. In ev'ry part
Is Hyperanthes active, ardent, seen
Throughout the huge battalion. He adjusts
Their equal range, then, cautious, lest on march
Their unaccustom'd order should relax,
Full in the centre of the foremost rank
Orontes plants, committing to his hand
Th' imperial standard; whose expanded folds

Glow'd in the air, presenting to the sun
The richest dye of Tyre. The royal bird
Amid the gorgeous tincture shone express'd
In high-embroider'd gold. The wary prince
On this conspicuous, leading, sign of war
Commands each satrap, posted in the van,
To fix his eye regardful, to direct
By this alone his even pace and slow,
Retiring, or advancing. So the star,
Chief of the spangles on that fancy'd bear,
Once an Idæan nymph, and nurse of Jove,
Bright Cynosura, to the Boreal pole
Attracts the sailor's eye, when distance hides
The headland signals, and her guiding ray,
New-ris'n, she throws. The hero next appoints
That ev'ry warrior through the length'ning files,
Observing none but those before him plac'd,
Shall watch their motions, and their steps pursue.
Nor is th' important thicket next the pass
Forgot. Two thousand of th' immortal guard
That station seize. His orders all perform'd,
Close by the standard he assumes his post.
Intrepid, thence he animates his friends—

' Heroic chieftains, whose unconquer'd force
Rebellious Ægypt and the Libyan felt,
Think what the splendour of your former deeds
From you exacts. Remember, from the great
Illustrious actions are a debt to fame.
No middle path remains for them to tread,
Whom she hath once ennobled. Lo! this day
By trophies new will signalize your names,
Or in dishonour will for ever cloud.'

He said, and vig'rous all to fight proceed.
As, when tempestuous Eurus stems the weight
Of western Neptune, struggling through the straits
Which bound Alcides' labours, here the storm
With rapid wing reverberates the tide;
There the contending surge, with furrow'd tops,
To mountains swells, and, whelming o'er the beach
On either coast, impels the hoary foam
On Mauritanian and Iberian strands:
Such is the dreadful onset. Persia keeps
Her foremost ranks unbroken, which are fill'd
By chosen warriors; while the num'rous crowd,
Though still promiscuous pouring from behind,

Give weight and pressure to th' embattled chiefs,
Despising danger. Like the mural strength
Of some proud city, bulwark'd round, and arm'd
With rising tow'rs, to guard her wealthy stores,
Immovable, impenetrable, stood
Laconia's ferry'd phalanx. In their face
Grim tyranny her threat'ning fetters shakes,
Red havock grinds, insatiable, his jaws.
Greece is behind, intrusting to their swords
Her laws, her freedom, and the sacred urns
Of their forefathers. Present now to thought
Their altars rise, the mansions of their birth,
Whate'er they honour, venerate, and love.

 Bright in the Persian van th' exalted lance
Of Hyperanthes flam'd. Beside him press'd
Abrocomes, Hydarnes, and the bulk
Of Abradates, terrible in war.
Firm, as a Memphian pyramid, was seen
Dieneces; while Agis, close in rank
With Menalippus, and the added strength
Of dauntless Maron, their connected shields
Upheld. Each unrelax'd array maintains

The conflict undecided; nor could Greece
Repel the adverse numbers, nor the weight
Of Asia's band select remove the Greeks.

Swift from Laconia's king, perceiving soon
The Persian's new arrangement, Medon flew,
Who thus the staid Dieneces address'd—

' Leonidas commands the Spartan ranks
To measure back some paces. Soon, he deems,
The unexperienc'd foes in wild pursuit
Will break their order. Then the charge renew.'

This heard, the signal of retreat is giv'n.
The Spartans seem to yield. The Persians stop.
Astonishment restrains them, and the doubt
Of unexpected victory. Their sloth
Abrocomes awakens—' By the sun,
They fly before us. My victorious friends,
Do you delay to enter Greece? Away!
Rush on intrepid! I already hear
Our horse, our chariots, thund'ring on her plains.
I see her temples wrapt in Persian fires.'

He spake. In hurry'd violence they roll
Tumultuous forward. All in headlong pace
Disjoin their order, and the line dissolve.
This when the sage Dieneces descries,
The Spartans halt, returning to the charge
With sudden vigour. In a moment, pierc'd
By his resistless steel, Orontes falls,
And quits th' imperial banner. This the chief
In triumph waves. The Spartans press the foe.
Close-wedg'd and square, in slow, progressive pace,
O'er heaps of mangled carcases and arms,
Invincible they tread. Composing flutes
Each thought, each motion, harmonize. No rage
Untunes their souls. The phalanx yet more deep
Of Medon follows; while the lighter bands
Glide by the flanks, and reach the broken foe.
Amid their flight what vengeance from the arm
Of Alpheus falls? O'er all in swift pursuit
Was he renown'd. His active feet had match'd
The son of Peleus in the dusty course;
But now the wrongs, the long-remember'd wrongs
Of Polydorus animate his strength
With tenfold vigour. Like th' empurpled moon,

When in eclipse her silver disk hath lost
The wonted light, his buckler's polish'd face
Is now obscur'd; the figur'd bosses drop
In crimson, spouting from his deathful strokes.
As when, with horror wing'd, a whirlwind rends
A shatter'd navy, from the ocean cast,
Enormous fragments hide the level beach;
Such as dejected Persia late beheld
On Thessaly's unnavigable strand:·
Thus o'er the champaign satraps lay bestrewn
By Alpheus, persevering in pursuit
Beyond the pass. Not Phœbus could inflict
On Niobè more vengeance when, incens'd
By her maternal arrogance, which scorn'd
Latona's race, he twang'd his ireful bow,
And one by one, from youth and beauty, hurl'd
Her sons to Pluto; nor severer pangs
That mother felt than pierc'd the gen'rous soul
Of Hyperanthes, while his noblest friends
On ev'ry side lay gasping. With despair
He still contends. Th' immortals, from their stand
Behind th' entangling thicket next the pass,
His signal rouses. Ere they clear their way

Well-caution'd Medon from the close defile
Two thousand Locrians pours. - An aspect new
The fight assumes. Through implicated shrubs
Confusion waves each banner. Falchions, spears,
And shields, are all encumber'd; till the Greeks
Had forc'd a passage to the yielding foe.
Then Medon's arm is felt. The dreadful boar,
Wide-wasting once the Calydonian fields,
In fury breaking from his gloomy lair,
Rang'd with less havock through unguarded folds
Than Medon, sweeping down the glitt'ring files,
So vainly styl'd immortal. From the cliff
Divine Melissa and Laconia's king
Enjoy the glories of Oïleus' son.
Fierce Alpheus too, returning from his chase,
Joins in the slaughter. Ev'ry Persian falls.

To him the Locrian chief—' Brave Spartan, thanks.
Through thee my purpose is accomplish'd full.
My phalanx here with levell'd rows of spears
Shall guard the shelter'd bushes. Come what may
From Asia's camp, th' assailant, flank'd and driv'n
Down yonder slope, shall perish. Gods of Greece,

You shall behold your fanes profusely deck'd
In splendid off'rings from Barbarian spoils,
Won by your free-born supplicants this day.'

  This said, he forms his ranks. Their threat'ning
    points
Gleam through the thicket, whence the shiv'ring foes
Avert their sight, like passengers dismay'd,
Who on their course by Nile's portentous banks
Descry, in ambush of perfidious reeds,
The crocodile's fell teeth. Contiguous lay
Thermopylæ. Dieneces secur'd
The narrow mouth. Two lines the Spartans shew'd:
One tow'rds the plain observ'd the Persian camp;
One, led by Agis, fac'd th' interior pass.

  Not yet discourag'd, Hyperanthes strives
The scatter'd host to rally. He exhorts,
Entreats; at length, indignant, thus exclaims—

  ' Degen'rate Persians! to sepulchral dust
Could breath return, your fathers from the tomb
Would utter groans. Inglorious, do ye leave

Behind you Persia's standard, to adorn
Some Grecian temple? Can your splendid cars,
Voluptuous couches, and delicious boards,
Your gold, your gems, ye satraps, be preserv'd
By cowardice and flight? The eunuch slave
Will scorn such lords, your women loath your beds.'

    Few hear him, fewer follow; while the fight
His unabating courage oft renews,
As oft repuls'd with danger; till, by all
Deserted, mixing in the gen'ral rout,
He yields to fortune, and regains the camp.
In short advances, thus the dying tide
Beats for a while against the shelving strand,
Still by degrees retiring, and at last
Within the bosom of the main subsides.

    Though Hyperanthes from the fight was driv'n;
Close to the mountain, whose indented side
There gave the widen'd pass an ample space
For numbers to embattle, still his post
Bold Intaphernes, underneath a cliff,
Against the firm Platæan line maintain'd.

On him look'd down Leonidas, like Death,
When, from his iron cavern call'd by Jove,
He stands gigantic on a mountain's head;
Whence he commands th' affrighted earth to quake,
And, crags and forests in his direful grasp
High-wielding, dashes on a town below,
Whose deeds of black impiety provoke
The long-enduring gods. Around the verge
Of Oeta, curving to a crescent's shape,
The marbles, timbers, fragments, lay amass'd.
The Helots, peasants, mariners, attend
In order nigh Leonidas. They watch
His look. He gives the signal. Rous'd at once,
The force, the skill, activity, and zeal,
Of thousands are combin'd. Down rush the piles.
Trees roll'd on trees, with mingled rock descend,
Unintermitted ruin. Loud resound
The hollow trunks against the mountain's side.
Swift bounds each craggy mass. The foes below
Look up aghast, in horror shrink, and die.
Whole troops, o'erwhelm'd beneath th' enormous load,
Lie hid and lost, as never they had known
A name or being. Intaphernes, clad

In regal splendour, progeny of kings,
Who rul'd Damascus and the Syrian palms,
Here slept for ever. Thousands of his train
In that broad space the ruins had not reach'd.
Back to their camp a passage they attempt
Through Lacedæmon's line. Them Agis stopt.
Before his pow'rful arm Pandates fell,
Sosarmes, Tachos. Menalippus dy'd
His youthful steel in blood. The mightier spear
Of Maron pierc'd battalions, and enlarg'd
The track of slaughter. Backward turn'd the rout,
Nor found a milder fate. Th' unweary'd swords
Of Dithyrambus and Diomedon,
Who from the hill are wheeling on their flank,
Still flash tremendous. To the shore they fly,
At once envelop'd by successive bands
Of diff'rent Grecians. From the gulph profound
Perdition here inevitable frowns,
While there, encircled by a grove of spears,
They stand devoted hecatombs to Mars.
Now not a moment's interval delays
Their gen'ral doom; but down the Malian steep
Prone are they hurry'd to th' expanded arms

Of horror, rising from the oozy deep,
And grasping all their numbers as they fall.
The dire confusion like a storm invades
The chafing surge. Whole troops Bellona rolls
In one vast ruin from the craggy ridge.
O'er all their arms, their ensigns, deep-engulph'd,
With hideous roar the waves for ever close.

LEONIDAS.

BOOK IX.

THE ARGUMENT.

Night coming on, the Grecians retire to their tents. A guard is placed on the Phocian wall, under the command of Agis. He admits into the camp a lady, accompanied by a single slave, and conducts them to Leonidas; when she discovers herself to be Ariana, sister of Xerxes and Hyperanthes, and sues for the body of Teribazus; which being found among the slain, she kills herself upon it. The slave, who attended her, proves to be Polydorus, brother to Alpheus and Maron, and who had been formerly carried into captivity by a Phœnician pirate. He relates, before an assembly of the chiefs, a message from Demaratus to the Spartans, which discloses the treachery of the Thebans, and of Epialtes the Malian, who had undertaken to lead part of the Persian army through a pass among the mountains of Oeta. This information throws the council into a great tumult, which is pacified by Leonidas, who sends Alpheus to observe the motions of these Persians, and Dieneces, with a party of Lacedæmonians, to support the Phocians, with whom the defence of these passages in the hills had been intrusted. In the mean time Agis sends the bodies of Teribazus and Ariana to the camp of Xerxes.

LEONIDAS.

BOOK IX.

In sable vesture, spangled o'er with stars,
The night assum'd her throne. Recall'd from war,
Their toil, protracted long, the Greeks forget,
Dissolv'd in silent slumber, all but those
Who watch th' uncertain perils of the dark,
A hundred warriors. Agis was their chief.
High on the wall, intent, the hero sat.
Fresh winds across the undulating bay
From Asia's host the various din convey'd
In one deep murmur, swelling on his ear;
When, by the sound of footsteps down the pass
Alarm'd, he calls aloud—' What feet are these
Which beat th' echoing pavement of the rock?
Reply, nor tempt inevitable fate.'

A voice reply'd—' No enemies we come,
But crave admittance in an humble tone.'

The Spartan answers—' Through the midnight shade
What purpose draws your wand'ring steps abroad ?'

To whom the stranger—' We are friends to Greece.
Through thy assistance we implore access
To Lacedæmon's king.' The cautious Greek
Still hesitates; when musically sweet
A tender voice his wond'ring ear allures.

' O gen'rous warrior, listen to the pray'r
Of one distress'd, whom grief alone hath led
Through midnight shades to these victorious tents;
A wretched woman, innocent of fraud.'

The chief, descending, through th' unfolded gates
Upheld a flaming torch. The light disclos'd
One first in servile garments. Near his side
A woman graceful and majestic stood;
Not with an aspect rivalling the pow'r
Of fatal Helen, or th' ensnaring charms

Of love's soft queen; but such as far surpass'd
Whate'er the lily, blending with the rose,
Spreads on the cheek of beauty, soon to fade;
Such as express'd a mind by wisdom rul'd,
By sweetness temper'd; virtue's purest light
Illumining the countenance divine:
Yet could not soften rig'rous fate, nor charm
Malignant fortune to revere the good;
Which oft with anguish rends a spotless heart,
And oft associates wisdom with despair.
In courteous phrase began the chief humane—

' Exalted fair, whose form adorns the night,
Forbear to blame the vigilance of war.
My slow compliance to the rigid laws
Of Mars impute. In me no longer pause
Shall from the presence of our king withhold
This thy apparent dignity and worth.'

Here ending, he conducts her. At the call
Of his lov'd brother, from his couch arose
Leonidas. In wonder he survey'd
Th' illustrious virgin, whom his presence aw'd.

Her eye, submissive, to the ground declin'd,
In veneration of the godlike man.
His mien, his voice, her anxious dread dispel,
Benevolent and hospitable, thus—

' Thy looks, fair stranger, amiable and great,
A mind delineate which from all commands
Supreme regard. Relate, thou noble dame,
By what relentless destiny compell'd,
Thy tender feet the paths of darkness tread;
Rehearse th' afflictions whence thy virtue mourns.'

On her wan cheek a sudden blush arose,
Like day first dawning on the twilight pale;
When, wrapt in grief, these words a passage found—

' If to be most unhappy, and to know
That hope is irrecoverably fled,
If to be great and wretched, may deserve
Commiseration from the brave; behold,
Thou glorious leader of unconquer'd bands,
Behold, descended from Darius' loins,
Th' afflicted Ariana; and my pray'r

Accept with pity, nor my tears disdain.
First, that I lov'd the best of human race,
Heroic, wise, adorn'd by ev'ry art,
Of shame unconscious, doth my heart reveal.
This day, in Grecian arms conspicuous clad,
He fought, he fell. A passion long conceal'd,
For me, alas! within my brother's arms
His dying breath resigning, he disclos'd.
Oh! I will stay my sorrows! will forbid
My eyes to stream before thee, and my breast,
O'erwhelm'd by anguish, will from sighs restrain!
For why should thy humanity be griev'd
At my distress, why learn from me to mourn
The lot of mortals, doom'd to pain and wo!
Hear then, O king, and grant my sole request,
To seek his body in the heaps of slain.'

Thus to the hero su'd the royal maid,
Resembling Ceres in majestic wo,
When supplicating Jove, from Stygian gloom,
And Pluto's black embraces, to redeem
Her lov'd and lost Proserpina. Awhile
On Ariana fixing steadfast eyes,
These tender thoughts Leonidas recall'd—

'Such are thy sorrows, O for ever dear,
Who now at Lacedæmon dost deplore
My everlasting absence!' Then aside.
He turn'd and sigh'd. Recov'ring, he address'd
His brother—' Most beneficent of men,
Attend, assist this princess!' Night retires
Before the purple-winged morn. A band
Is call'd. The well-remember'd spot they find
Where Teribazus from his dying hand
Dropt in their sight his formidable sword.
Soon from beneath a pile of Asian dead
They draw the hero, by his armour known.

Then, Ariana, what transcending pangs
Were thine! what horrors! In thy tender breast
Love still was mightiest. On the bosom cold
Of Teribazus, grief-distracted maid,
Thy beauteous limbs were thrown. Thy snowy hue
The clotted gore disfigur'd. On his wounds
Loose flow'd thy hair, and, bubbling from thy eyes,
Impetuous sorrow lav'd th' empurpled clay.
When forth in groans these lamentations broke—

'O, torn for ever from these weeping eyes!

Thou, who, despairing to obtain a heart
Which then most lov'd thee, didst untimely yield
Thy life to fate's inevitable dart
For her, who now in agony reveals
Her tender passion, who repeats her vows
To thy deaf ear, who fondly to her own
Unites thy cheek insensible and cold.
Alas! do those unmoving, ghastly, orbs
Perceive my gushing sorrow? Can that heart
At my complaint dissolve the ice of death,
To share my suff'rings? Never, never more
Shall Ariana bend a list'ning ear
To thy enchanting eloquence, nor feast
Her mind on wisdom from thy copious tongue!
Oh! bitter, insurmountable distress!'

 She could no more. Invincible despair
Suppress'd all utt'rance. As a marble form,
Fix'd on the solemn sepulchre, inclines
The silent head, in imitated wo,
O'er some dead hero whom his country lov'd,
Entranc'd by anguish, o'er the breathless clay
So hung the princess. On the gory breach,

Whence life had issu'd by the fatal blow,
Mute for a space, and motionless, she gaz'd;
When thus in accents firm. ' Imperial pomp,
Foe to my quiet, take my last farewell!
There is a state where only virtue holds
The rank supreme. My Teribazus there
From his high order must descend to mine.'

Then, with no trembling hand, no change of look,
She drew a poniard, which her garment veil'd;
And, instant sheathing in her heart the blade,
On her slain lover silent sunk in death!
The unexpected stroke prevents the care
Of Agis, pierc'd by horror and distress,
Like one who, standing on a stormy beach,
Beholds a found'ring vessel by the deep
At once engulph'd, his pity feels and mourns,
Depriv'd of pow'r to save; so Agis view'd
The prostrate pair. He dropt a tear, and thus—

' Oh, much lamented! Heavy on your heads
Hath evil fall'n, which o'er your pale remains
Commands this sorrow from a stranger's eye.

Then with no trembling hand, no change of look,
She drew a poniard, which her garment veil'd;
And, instant sheathing in her heart the blade,
On her slain lover silent sunk in death.

Illustrious ruins! May the grave impart
That peace which life deny'd! And now receive
This pious office from a hand unknown.'

He spake, unclasping from his shoulders broad
His ample robe. He strew'd the waving folds
O'er each wan visage, turning then, address'd
The slave, in mute dejection standing near—

' Thou, who, attendant on this hapless fair,
Hast view'd this dreadful spectacle, return.
These bleeding reliques bear to Persia's king;
Thou with four captives, whom I free from bonds.'

' Art thou a Spartan?' interrupts the slave.
' Dost thou command me to return, and pine
In climes unbless'd by liberty or laws?
Grant me to see Leonidas. Alone
Let him decide if, wretched as I seem,
I may not claim protection from this camp.'

' Who'er thou art,' rejoins the chief, amaz'd,
But not offended, ' thy ignoble garb

Conceal'd a spirit which I now revere.
Thy countenance demands a better lot
Than I, a stranger to thy hidden worth,
Unconscious, offer'd. Freedom dwells in Greece,
Humanity and justice. Thou shalt see
Leonidas, their guardian.' To the king
He leads him straight; presents him in these words—

' In mind superior to the base attire
Which marks his limbs with shame, a stranger comes,
Who thy protection claims.' The slave subjoins—

' I stand thy suppliant now. Thou soon shalt learn
If I deserve thy favour. I request
To meet th' assembled chieftains of this host.
Oh! I am fraught with tidings which import
The weal of ev'ry Grecian.' Agis swift,
Appointed by Leonidas, convenes
The diff'rent leaders. To the tent they speed.
Before them call'd, the stranger thus began—

' O Alpheus! Maron! Hither turn your sight,
And know your brother!' From their seats they start.

From either breaks, in ecstasy, the name
Of Polydorus. To his dear embrace
Each fondly strives to rush; but he withstands;
While down his cheek a flood of anguish pours
From his dejected eyes, in torture bent
On that vile garb, dishonouring his form.
At length these accents, intermix'd with groans,
A passage found, while mute attention gaz'd.

' You first should know if this unhappy slave
Yet merits your embraces.' Then approach'd
Leonidas. Before him all recede,
Ev'n Alpheus' self, and yields his brother's hand,
Which in his own the regal hero press'd.
Still Polydorus on his gloomy front
Repugnance stern to consolation bore;
When thus the king with majesty benign—

' Lo! ev'ry heart is open to thy worth.
Injurious fortune and enfeebling time,
By servitude and grief, severely try
A lib'ral spirit. Try'd, but not subdu'd,
Dost thou appear. Whatever be our lot

Is heav'n's appointment.   Patience best becomes
The citizen and soldier.   Let the sight
Of friends and brethren dissipate thy gloom.'

Of men the gentlest, Agis too advanc'd,
Who with increas'd humanity began—

' Now in thy native liberty secure,
Smile on thy past affliction, and relate
What chance restores thy merit to the arms
Of friends and kindred.'   Polydorus then—

' I was a Spartan.   When my tender prime
On manhood border'd, from Laconia's shores
Snatch'd by Phœnician pirates, I was sold
A slave, by Hyperanthes bought, and giv'n
To Ariana.   Gracious was her hand.
But I remain'd a bondman, still estrang'd
From Lacedæmon.   Demaratus oft,
In friendly sorrow, would my lot deplore;
Nor less his own ill-fated virtue mourn'd,
Lost to his country in a servile court,
The center of corruption; where in smiles
Are painted envy, treachery, and hate,

With rankling malice; where, alone sincere,
The dissolute seek no disguise; where those,
Possessing all a monarch can bestow,
Are far less happy than the meanest heir
To freedom, far more grov'ling than the slave
Who serves their cruel pride. Yet here the sun
Ten times his yearly circle hath renew'd
Since Polydorus hath in bondage groan'd.
My bloom is pass'd, or, pining in despair,
Untimely wither'd. I at last return
A messenger of fate, who tidings bear
Of desolation.' Here he paus'd in grief
Redoubled; when Leonidas—' Proceed.
Should from thy lips inevitable death
To all be threaten'd, thou art heard by none
Whose dauntless hearts can entertain a thought
But how to fall the noblest.' Thus the king.
The rest in speechless expectation wait.
Such was the solemn silence which o'erspread
The shrine of Ammon, or Dodona's shades,
When anxious mortals from the mouth of Jove
Their doom explor'd. Nor Polydorus long
Suspends the counsel, but resumes his tale—

' As I this night accompany'd the steps
Of Ariana, near the pass we saw
A restless form, now traversing the way,
Now as a statue rivetted by doubt,
Then on a sudden starting to renew
An eager pace. As nearer we approach'd,
He by the moon, which glimmer'd on our heads,
Descry'd us. Straight advancing, whither bent
Our midnight course he ask'd. I knew the voice
Of Demaratus. To my breast I clasp'd
The venerable exile, and reply'd—
" Laconia's camp we seek. Demand no more.
Farewell." He wept. " Be heav'n thy guide," he said,
" Thrice happy Polydorus. Thou again
Mayst visit Sparta, to these eyes deny'd.
Soon as arriv'd at those triumphant tents,
Say to the Spartans, from their exil'd king,
Although their blind credulity depriv'd
The wretched Demaratus of his home,
From ev'ry joy secluded, from his wife,
His offspring torn, his countrymen and friends,
Him from his virtue they could ne'er divide.
Say that ev'n here, where all are kings or slaves,

Amid the riot of flagitious courts,
Not quite extinct, his Spartan spirit glows,
Though grief hath dimm'd its fires. Rememb'ring this,
Report that newly to the Persian host
Return'd a Malian, Epialtes nam'd,
Who, as a spy, the Grecian tents had sought.
He to the monarch magnify'd his art,
Which, by delusive eloquence, had wrought
The Greeks to such despair, that ev'ry band
To Persia's sov'reign standard would have bow'd,
Had not the spirit of a single chief,
By fear unconquer'd, and on death resolv'd,
Restor'd their valour: therefore, would the king
Trust to his guidance a selected force;
They soon should pierce th' unguarded bounds of Greece
Through a neglected aperture above,
Where no Leonidas should bar their way:
Meantime by him the treach'rous Thebans sent
Assurance of their aid. Th' assenting prince
At once decreed two myriads to advance
With Hyperanthes. Ev'ry lord besides,
Whom youth, or courage, or ambition warm,
Rous'd by the traitor's eloquence, attend

From all the nations, with a rival zeal
To enter Greece the foremost." In a sigh
He clos'd—like me.' Tremendous, from his seat
Uprose Diomedon. His eyes were flames.
When swift, on trembling Anaxander, broke
These ireful accents from his livid lips—

' Yet, ere we fall, O traitor, shall this arm
To hell's avenging furies sink thy head!'

All now is tumult. Ev'ry bosom swells
With wrath untam'd, and vengeance. Half unsheath'd,
Th' impetuous falchion of Platæa flames.
But, as the Colchian sorceress, renown'd
In legends old, or Circé, when they fram'd
A potent spell, to smoothness charm'd the main,
And lull'd Æolian rage by mystic song,
Till not a billow heav'd against the shore,
Nor ev'n the wanton-winged zephyr breath'd
The lightest whisper through the magic air;
So, when thy voice, Leonidas, is heard,
Confusion listens; ire in silent awe
Subsides. ' Withhold this rashness,' cries the king.

' To proof of guilt let punishment succeed.
Not yet Barbarian shouts our camp alarm.
We still have time for vengeance, time to know
If menac'd ruin we may yet repel,
Or how most glorious perish.'   Next arose
Dieneces, and thus th' experienc'd man—

' Ere they surmount our fences Xerxes' troops
Must learn to conquer, and the Greeks to fly.
The spears of Phocis guard that secret pass.
To them let instant messengers depart,
And note the hostile progress.'   Alpheus here—

' Leonidas, behold, my willing feet
Shall to the Phocians bear thy high commands;
Shall climb the hill to watch th' approaching foe.'

' Thou active son of valour,' quick returns
The chief of Lacedæmon, ' in my thoughts
For ever present, when the public weal
Requires the swift, the vigilant, and bold,
Go, climb, surmount the rock's aerial height;
Observe the hostile march.   A Spartan band,

Dieneces, provide. Thyself conduct
Their speedy succour to our Phocian friends.'

 The council rises. For his course prepar'd,
While day, declining, prompts his eager feet,
' O Polydorus,' Alpheus thus in haste,
' Long lost, and late recover'd, we must part
Again, perhaps for ever. Thou return
To kiss the sacred soil which gave thee birth,
And calls thee back to freedom. Brother dear,
I should have sighs to give thee—but farewell!
My country chides me, loit'ring in thy arms.'

 This said, he darts along, nor looks behind,
When Polydorus answers—' Alpheus, no.
I have the marks of bondage to erase.
My blood must wash the shameful stain away.'

 ' We have a father,' Maron interpos'd.
' Thy unexpected presence will revive
His heavy age, now childless and forlorn.'

 To him the brother with a gloomy frown—

' Ill should I comfort others. View these eyes;
Faint is their light; and vanish'd was my bloom
Before its hour of ripeness. In my breast
Grief will retain a mansion, nor by time
Be dispossess'd. Unceasing shall my soul
Brood o'er the black remembrance of my youth
In slavery exhausted. Life to me
Hath lost its savour.' Then, in sullen wo,
His head declines. His brother pleads in vain.

 Now in his view Dieneces appear'd,
With Sparta's band. Immoveable, his eyes
On them he fix'd, revolving these dark thoughts—

 ' I too, like them, from Lacedæmon spring;
Like them instructed once to poise the spear,
To lift the pond'rous shield. Ill-destin'd wretch!
Thy arm is grown enervate, and would sink
Beneath a buckler's weight. Malignant fates!
Who have compell'd my free-born hand to change
The warrior's arms for ignominious bonds!
Would you compensate for my chains, my shame,
My ten years' anguish, and the fell despair

Which on my youth have prey'd? Relenting once,
Grant I may bear my buckler to the field,
And, known a Spartan, seek the shades below.'

' Why, to be known a Spartan, must thou seek
The shades below?' Impatient Maron spake.
' Live, and be known a Spartan by thy deeds.
Live, and enjoy thy dignity of birth.
Live, and perform the duties which become
A citizen of Sparta. Still thy brow
Frowns gloomy, still unyielding. He, who leads
Our band, all fathers of a noble race,
Will ne'er permit thy barren day to close
Without an offspring to uphold the state.'

' He will,' replies the brother in a glow,
Prevailing o'er the paleness of his cheek;
' He will permit me to complete by death
The measure of my duty; will permit
Me to achieve a service, which no hand
But mine can render, to adorn his fall
With double lustre, strike the harb'rous foe
With endless terror, and avenge the shame

Of an enslav'd Laconian.'   Closing here
His words mysterious, quick he turn'd away,
To find the tent of Agis.   There his hand
In grateful sorrow minister'd her aid;
While the humane, the hospitable, care
Of Agis, gently by her lover's corse,
On one sad bier, the pallid beauties laid
Of Ariana.   He from bondage freed
Four eastern captives, whom his gen'rous arm
That day had spar'd in battle; then began
This solemn charge.   ' You, Persians, whom my sword
Acquir'd in war, unransom'd, shall depart.
To you I render freedom, which you sought
To wrest from me.   One recompense I ask,
And one alone.   Transport to Asia's camp
This bleeding princess.   Bid the Persian king
Weep o'er this flow'r, untimely cut in bloom;
Then say th' all-judging pow'rs have thus ordain'd.
Thou, whose ambition o'er the groaning earth
Leads desolation; o'er the nations spreads
Calamity and tears; thou first shalt mourn,
And through thy house destruction first shall range.'

Dismiss'd, they gain the rampart, where on guard
Was Dithyrambus posted. He perceiv'd
The mournful bier approach. To him the fate
Of Ariana was already told.
He met the captives with a moisten'd eye,
Full bent on Teribazus, sigh'd, and spake—

' O that, assuming with those Grecian arms
A Grecian spirit, thou in scorn hadst look'd
On princes! Worth like thine, from slavish courts
Withdrawn, had ne'er been wasted to support
A king's injustice. Then a gentler lot
Had blest thy life, or, dying, thou hadst known,
How sweet is death for liberty. A Greek
Affords these friendly wishes, though his head
Had lost the honours gather'd from thy fall,
When fortune favour'd, or propitious Jove
Smil'd on the better cause. Ill-fated pair,
Whom in compassion's purest dew I lave,
But that my hand infix'd the deathful wound,
And must be grievous to your loathing shades,
From all the neighb'ring vallies would I cull
Their fairest growth to strew your hearse with flow'rs.

Yet, O accept these tears and pious pray'rs!
May peace surround your ashes! May your shades
Pass o'er the silent pool to happier seats!'

He ceas'd in tears. The captives leave the wall,
And slowly down Thermopylæ proceed.

LEONIDAS.

BOOK X.

THE ARGUMENT.

Medon convenes the Locrian commanders, and harangues them; repairs at midnight to his sister Melissa in the temple, and receives from her the first intelligence that the Persians were in actual possession of the upper Straits, which had been abandoned by the Phocians. Melibœus brings her tidings of her father's death. She strictly enjoins her brother to preserve his life by a timely retreat, and recommends the enforcement of her advice to the prudence and zeal of Melibœus. In the morning the bodies of Teribazus and Ariana are brought into the presence of Xerxes, soon after a report had reached the camp that great part of his navy was shipwrecked. The Persian monarch, quite dispirited, is persuaded by Argestes to send an ambassador to the Spartan king. Argestes himself is deputed, who, after revealing his embassy in secret to Leonidas, is by him led before the whole army, and there receives his answer. Alpheus returns, and declares that the enemy was master of the passages in the hills, and would arrive at Thermopylæ the next morning; upon which Leonidas offers to send away all the troops, except his three hundred Spartans; but Diomedon, Demophilus, Dithyrambus, and Megistias, refuse to depart: then, to relieve the perplexity of Medon on this occasion, he transfers to him the supreme command, dismisses Argestes, orders the companions of his own fate to be ready in arms by sunset, and retires to his pavilion.

LEONIDAS.

BOOK X.

THE Grecian leaders, from the counsel ris'n,
Among the troops dispersing, by their words,
Their looks undaunted, warm the coldest heart
Against new dangers threat'ning. To his tent
The Locrian captains Medon swift convenes,
Exhorting thus—' O, long-approv'd my friends,
You, who have seen my father in the field
Triumphant, bold assistants of my arm
In labours not inglorious, who this day
Have rais'd fresh trophies, be prepar'd. If help
Be further wanted in the Phocian camp,
You will the next be summon'd. Locris lies
To ravage first expos'd. Your ancient fane,
Your goddesses, your priestess half-ador'd,

The daughter of Oïleus, from your swords
Protection claim against an impious foe.'

All anxious for Melissa, he dismiss'd
Th' applauding vet'rans; to the sacred cave
Then hasten'd. Under heav'n's night-shaded cope
He mus'd. Melissa in her holy place
How to approach, with inauspicious steps,
How to accost, his pensive mind revolv'd:
When Mycon, pious vassal of the fane,
Descending through the cavern, at the sight
Of Medon stopt, and thus—' Thy presence, lord,
The priestess calls. To Lacedæmon's king
I bear a message, suff'ring no delay.'

He quits the chief, whose rapid feet ascend,
Soon ent'ring where the pedestal displays
Thy form, Calliopè sublime. The lyre,
Whose accents immortality confer,
Thy fingers seem to wake. On either side
The snowy gloss of Parian marble shews
Four of thy sisters through surrounding shade.
Before each image is a virgin plac'd.

Before each virgin dimly burns a lamp,
Whose livid spires just temper with a gleam
The dead obscurity of night. Apart
The priestess thoughtful sits. Thus Medon breaks
The solemn silence—' Anxious for thy state,
Without a summons, to thy pure abode
I was approaching. Deities who know
The present, past, and future, let my lips
Unblam'd have utt'rance! Thou, my sister, hear!
Thy breast let wisdom strengthen. Impious foes
Through Oeta now are passing.' She replies—

' Are passing, brother! They, alas, are pass'd,
Are in possession of the upper Strait!
Hear in thy turn. A dire narration hear.
A favour'd goat, conductor of my herd,
Stray'd to a dale, whose outlet is the post
To Phocians left, and penetrates to Greece.
Him Mycon following, by a hostile band,
Light arm'd forerunners of a num'rous host,
Was seiz'd. By fear of menac'd torments forc'd,
He shew'd a passage up that mountain's side
Whose length of wood o'ershades the Phocian land.

To dry and sapless trunks in diff'rent parts
Fire, by the Persians artfully apply'd,
Soon grew to flames. This done, the troop return'd,
Detaining Mycon. Now the mountain blaz'd.
The Phocians, ill-commanded, left their post,
Alarm'd, confus'd. More distant ground they chose.
In blind delusion forming there, they spread
Their ineffectual banners, to repel
Imagin'd peril from those fraudful lights,
By stratagem prepar'd. A real foe
Meantime secur'd the undefended pass.
This Mycon saw. Escaping thence to me,
He, by my orders, hastens to inform
Leonidas.' She paus'd. Like one, who sees
The forked lightning into shivers rive
A knotted oak, or crumble tow'rs to dust,
Aghast was Medon; then, recov'ring, spake—

' Thou boasted glory of th' Oïlean house,
If e'er thy brother bow'd in rev'rence due
To thy superior virtues, let his voice
Be now regarded. From th' endanger'd fane,
My sister, fly. Whatever be my lot,

A troop select of Locrians shall transport
Thy sacred person where thy will ordains.'

' Think not of me,' returns the dame. ' To Greece
Direct thy zeal. My peasants are conven'd,
That by their labour, when the fatal hour
Requires, with massy fragments I may bar
That cave to human entrance. Best belov'd
Of brothers, now a serious ear incline.
Awhile in Greece, to fortune's wanton gale,
His golden banner shall the Persian king,
Deluded, wave. Leonidas, by death
Preserving Sparta, will his spirit leave
To blast the glitt'ring pageant. Medon, live
To share that glory. Thee to perish here
No law, no oracle, enjoins. To die,
Uncall'd, is blameful. Let thy pious hand
Secure Oïleus from Barbarian force.
To Sparta, mindful of her noble host,
Entrust his rev'rend head.' Th' assembled hinds,
Youths, maidens, wives with nurselings at their breasts,
Around her now in consternation stood,
The women weeping, mute, aghast the men.

To them she turns—' You never, faithful race,
Your priestess shall forsake. Melissa here,
Despairing never of the public weal,
For better days in solitude shall wait,
Shall cheer your sadness. My prophetic soul
Sees through time's cloud the liberty of Greece
More stable, more effulgent. In his blood
Leonidas cements th' unshaken base
Of that strong tow'r, which Athens shall exalt
To cast a shadow o'er the eastern world.'

This utter'd, tow'rd the temple's inmost seat
Of sanctity her solemn step she bends,
Devout, enraptur'd. In their dark'ning lamps
The pallid flames are fainting. Dim through mists
The morning peeps. An awful silence reigns.
While Medon pensive from the fane descends,
But instant reappears. Behind him close
Treads Melibœus, through the cavern's mouth
Ascending, pale in aspect; not unlike
What legends tell of spectres, by the force
Of necromantic sorcery constrain'd;
Through earth's dark bowels, which the spell disjoin'd,

They from death's mansion, in reluctant sloth,
Rose to divulge the secrets of their graves,
Or mysteries of fate. His cheerful brow,
O'erclouded, paleness on his healthful cheek,
A dull, unwonted heaviness of pace,
Portend disast'rous tidings. Medon spake—

' Turn, holy sister. By the gods belov'd,
May they sustain thee in this mournful hour.
Our father, good Oïleus, is no more!'
' Rehearse thy tidings, swain.' He takes the word—

' Thou wast not present when his mind, outstretch'd
By zeal for Greece, transported by his joy
To entertain Leonidas, refus'd
Due rest. Old age his ardour had forgot,
To his last waking moment with his guest
In rapt'rous talk redundant. He at last,
Compos'd and smiling in th' embrace of sleep,
To Pan's protection at the island fane
Was left. He wak'd no more. The fatal news,
To you discover'd, from the chiefs I hide.'

Melissa heard, inclin'd her forehead low

Before th' insculptur'd deities. A sigh
Broke from her heart, these accents from her lips—

' The full of days and honours through the gate
Of painless slumber is retir'd. His tomb
Shall stand among his fathers, in the shade
Of his own trophies. Placid were his days,
Which flow'd through blessings. As a river pure,
Whose sides are flow'ry, and whose meadows fair,
Meets in his course a subterranean void;
There dips his silver head, again to rise,
And, rising, glide through flow'rs and meadows new;
So shall Oïleus, in those happier fields
Where never tempests roar, nor humid clouds
In mists dissolve, nor white-descending flakes
Of winter violate th' eternal green;
Where never gloom of trouble shades the mind,
Nor gust of passion heaves the quiet breast,
Nor dews of grief are sprinkled. Thou art gone,
Host of divine Leonidas on earth!
Art gone before him to prepare the feast,
Immortalizing virtue.' Silent here,
Around her head she wraps her hallow'd pall.

Her prudent virgins interpose a hymn,
Not in a plaintive, but majestic flow,
To which their fingers, sweeping o'er the chords,
The lyre's full tone attemper. She unveils;
Then, with a voice, a countenance, compos'd—

' Go, Medon, pillar of th' Oïlean house.
New cares, new duties, claim thy precious life.
Perform the pious obsequies. Let tears,
Let groans, be absent from the sacred dust
Which heav'n in life so favour'd, more in death.
A term of righteous days, an envy'd urn,
Like his, for Medon is Melissa's pray'r.
Thou, Melibœus, cordial, high in rank
Among the prudent, warn and watch thy lord.
My benediction shall reward thy zeal.'

Sooth'd by the blessings of such perfect lips,
They both depart. And now the climbing sun
To Xerxes' tent discover'd from afar
The Persian captives with their mournful load.
Before them rumour, through her sable trump,
Breathes lamentation. Horror lends his voice

To spread the tidings of disastrous fate
Along Spercheos. As a vapour black,
Which from the distant, horizontal verge
Ascending, nearer still and nearer bends
To higher lands its progress, there condens'd,
Throws darkness o'er the valleys, while the face
Of nature saddens round; so, step by step,
In motion slow, th' advancing bier diffus'd
A solemn sadness o'er the camp. A hedge
Of trembling spears on either hand is form'd.
Tears, underneath his iron-pointed cone,
The Sacian drops. The Caspian savage feels
His heart transpierc'd, and wonders at the pain.
In Xerxes' presence are the bodies plac'd;
Nor he forbids. His agitated breast
All night had weigh'd against his future hopes
His present losses, his defeated ranks,
By myriads thinn'd, their multitude abash'd,
His fleet thrice-worsted, torn by storms, reduc'd
To half its number. When he slept, in dreams
He saw the haggard dead, which floated round
Th' adjoining strands. Disasters new their ghosts
In sullen frowns, in shrill upbraidings, bode.

Thus, ere the gory bier approach'd his eyes,
He in dejection had already lost
His kingly pride, the parent of disdain
And cold indifference to human woes.
Not ev'n beside his sister's nobler corse
Her humble lover could awake his scorn.
The captives told their piercing tale. He heard;
He felt awhile compassion. But ere long
Those traces vanish'd from the tyrant's breast.
His former gloom redoubles. For himself
His anxious bosom heaves, oppress'd by fear,
Lest he, with all his splendour, should be cast
A prey to fortune. Thoughtful near the throne
Laconia's exile waits, to whom the king—

' O Demaratus, what will fate ordain?
Lo! fortune turns against me. What shall check
Her further malice, when her daring stride
Invades my house with ravage, and profanes
The blood of great Darius? I have sent
From my unguarded side the chosen band,
My bravest chiefs, to pass the desert hill;
Have to the conduct of a Malian spy

My hopes intrusted. May not there the Greeks,
In opposition more tremendous still,
More ruinous, than yester sun beheld,
Maintain their post invincible, renew
Their stony thunder in augmented rage,
And send whole quarries down the craggy steeps,
Again to crush my army? Oh! unfold
Thy secret thoughts, nor hide the harshest truth.
Say, what remains to hope?' The exile here—

' Too well, O monarch, do thy fears presage
What may befall thy army. If the Greeks,
Arrang'd within Thermopylæ, a pass
Accessible and practis'd, could repel
With such destruction their unnumber'd foes,
What scenes of havock may untrodden paths,
Confin'd among the craggy hills, afford?'

Lost in despair, the monarch silent sat.
Not less unmann'd than Xerxes, from his place
Uprose Argestes; but, concealing fear,
These artful words deliver'd—' If the king,
Propitious, wills to spare his faithful bands,

Nor spread at large the terrors of his pow'r,
More gentle means of conquest than by arms,
Nor less secure, may artifice supply.
Renown'd Dárius, thy immortal sire,
Bright in the spoil of kingdoms, long in vain
The fields of proud Euphrates with his host
O'erspread. At length, confiding in the wiles
Of Zopyrus, the mighty prince subdu'd
The Babylonian ramparts. Who shall count
The thrones and states by stratagem o'erturn'd?
But, if corruption join her pow'rful aid,
Not one can stand. What race of men possess
That probity, that wisdom, which the veil
Of craft shall never blind, nor proffer'd wealth,
Nor splendid pow'r, seduce? O Xerxes, born
To more than mortal greatness, canst thou find,
Through thy unbounded sway, no dazzling gift
Which may allure Leonidas? Dispel
The cloud of sadness from those sacred eyes.
Great Monarch, proffer to Laconia's chief
What may thy own magnificence declare,
And win his friendship. O'er his native Greece
Invest him sov'reign. Thus procure his sword

For thy succeeding conquests.'   Xerxes here,
As from a trance awak'ning, swift replies—

' Wise are thy dictates.   Fly to Sparta's chief.
Argestes, fall before him.   Bid him join
My arms, and reign o'er ev'ry Grecian state.'

He scarce had finish'd when in haste approach'd
Artuchus.   Startled at the ghastly stage
Of death, that guardian of the Persian fair
Thus in a groan—' Thou deity malign,
O Arimanius, what a bitter draught
For my sad lips thy cruelty hath mix'd!
Is this the flow'r of women, to my charge
So lately giv'n?   Oh! princess, I have rang'd
The whole Sperchean valley, woods and caves,
In quest of thee, found here a lifeless corse.
Astonishment and horror lock my tongue.'

Pride now, reviving in the monarch's breast,
Dispell'd his black despondency awhile,
With gall more black effacing from his heart
Each merciful impression.   Stern he spake—

'Remove her, satrap, to the female train.
Let them the due solemnities perform.
But never she, by Mithra's light I swear,
Shall sleep in Susa with her kindred dust,
Who by ignoble passions hath debas'd
The blood of Xerxes. Greece beheld her shame;
Let Greece behold her tomb. The low-born slave,
Who dar'd to Xerxes' sister lift his hopes,
On some bare crag expose.' The Spartan here—

'My royal patron, let me speak—and die,
If such thy will. This cold, disfigur'd clay
Was late thy soldier, gallantly who fought,
Who nobly perish'd, long the dearest friend
Of Hyperanthes, hazarding his life
Now in thy cause. O'er Persians thou dost reign;
None more than Persians venerate the brave!'

'Well hath he spoke,' Artuchus firm subjoins.
'But, if the king his rigour will inflict
On this dead warrior, Heav'n o'erlook the deed,
Nor on our heads accumulate fresh woes!
The shatter'd fleet, th' intimidated camp,

The band select, through Oeta's dang'rous wilds
At this dread crisis struggling, must obtain
Support from heav'n, or Asia's glory falls.'

Fell pride, recoiling at these awful words
In Xerxes' frozen bosom, yields to fear,
Resuming there the sway. He grants the corse
To Demaratus. Forth Artuchus moves
Behind the bier, uplifted by his train.

Argestes, parted from his master's side,
Ascends a car; and, speeding o'er the beach,
Sees Artemisia. She the ashes pale
Of slaughter'd Carians, on the pyre consum'd,
Was then collecting for the fun'ral vase
In exclamation thus—' My subjects, lost
On earth, descend to happier climes below—
The fawning, dastard counsellors, who left
Your worth deserted in the hour of need,
May kites disfigure, may the wolf devour—
Shade of my husband, thou salute in smiles
These gallant warriors, faithful once to thee,
Nor less to me. They tidings will report

Of Artemisia, to revive thy love—
May wretches like Argestes never clasp
Their wives, their offspring! Never greet their homes!
May their unbury'd limbs dismiss their ghosts
To wail for ever on the banks of Styx!'

  Then, turning tow'rd her son—' Come, virtuous boy,
Let us transport these reliques of our friends
To yon tall bark, in pendent sable clad.
They, if her keel be destin'd to return,
Shall in paternal monuments repose.
Let us embark. Till Xerxes shuts his ear
To false Argestes, in her vessel hid,
Shall Artemisia's gratitude lament
Her bounteous sov'reign's fate. Leander, mark.
The Doric virtues are not eastern plants.
Them foster still within thy gen'rous breast;
But keep in covert from the blaze of courts;
Where flattery's guile, in oily words profuse,
In action tardy, o'er th' ingenuous tongue,
The arm of valour, and the faithful heart,
Will ever triumph. Yet my soul enjoys
Her own presage, that destiny reserves

An hour for my revenge.' Concluding here,
She gains the fleet. Argestes sweeps along
On rapid wheels from Artemisia's view;
Like night, protectress foul of heinous deeds,
With treason, rape, and murder, at her heel,
Before the eye of morn retreating swift,
To hide her loathsome visage. Soon he reach'd
Thermopylæ; descending from his car,
Was led by Dithyrambus to the tent
Of Sparta's ruler. Since the fatal news
By Mycon late deliver'd, he apart
With Polydorus had consulted long
On high attempts; and, now sequester'd, sat
To ruminate on vengeance. At his feet
Prone fell the satrap, and began—' The will
Of Xerxes bends me prostrate to the earth
Before thy presence. Great and matchless chief,
Thus says the lord of Asia, " Join my arms;
Thy recompense is Greece. Her fruitful plains,
Her gen'rous steeds, her flocks, her num'rous towns,
Her sons, I render to thy sov'reign hand."
And, O illustrious warrior, heed my words.
Think on the bliss of royalty, the pomp

Of courts, their endless pleasures, trains of slaves,
Who restless watch for thee and thy delights.
Think on the glories of unrivall'd sway.
Look on th' Ionic, on th' Æolian Greeks.
From them their phantom liberty is flown;
While in each province, rais'd by Xerxes' pow'r,
Some favour'd chief presides; exalted state,
Ne'er giv'n by envious freedom. On his head
He bears the gorgeous diadem; he sees
His equals once in adoration stoop
Beneath his footstool. What superior beams
Will from thy temples blaze, when gen'ral Greece,
In noblest states abounding, calls thee lord,
Thee only worthy! How will each rejoice
Around thy throne, and hail th' auspicious day
When thou, distinguish'd by the Persian king,
Didst in thy sway consenting nations bless,
Didst calm the fury of unsparing war,
Which else had delug'd all with blood and flames!'

Leonidas replies not, but commands
The Thespian youth, still watchful near the tent,
To summon all the Grecians. He obeys.

The king uprises from his seat, and bids
The Persian follow. He, amaz'd, attends,
Surrounded soon by each assembling band;
When thus at length the godlike Spartan spake—

' Here, Persian, tell thy embassy. Repeat
That, to obtain my friendship, Asia's prince
To me hath proffer'd sov'reignty o'er Greece.
Then view these bands, whose valour shall preserve
That Greece unconquer'd which your king bestows;
Shall strew your bodies on her crimson'd plains.
The indignation, painted on their looks,
Their gen'rous scorn, may answer for their chief.
Yet from Leonidas, thou wretch, inur'd
To vassalage and baseness, hear.—The pomp,
The arts of pleasure in despotic courts,
I spurn, abhorrent! In a spotless heart
I look for pleasure. I from righteous deeds
Derive my splendour. No adoring crowd,
No purpled slaves, no mercenary spears,
My state embarrass. I in Sparta rule
By laws, my rulers, with a guard unknown
To Xerxes, public confidence and love.

Here Persian tell thy embassy —

Leonidas. Book X

No pale suspicion of th' empoison'd bowl,
Th' assassin's poniard, or provok'd revolt,
Chase from my decent couch the peace deny'd
To his resplendent canopy. Thy king,
Who hath profan'd by proffer'd bribes my ear,
Dares not to meet my arm. Thee, trembling slave,
Whose embassy was treason, I despise,
And therefore spare.' Diomedon subjoins—

' Our marble temples these Barbarians waste,
A crime less impious than a bare attempt
Of sacrilege on virtue! Grant my suit,
Thou living temple, where the goddess dwells.
To me consign the caitiff. Soon the winds
Shall parch his limbs on Oeta's tallest pine.'

Amidst his fury suddenly return'd
The speed of Alpheus. All, suspended, fix'd
On him their eyes, impatient. He began—

' I am return'd a messenger of ill.
Close to the passage, op'ning into Greece,
That post committed to the Phocian guard,

O'erhangs a bushy cliff. A station there
Behind the shrubs by dead of night I took,
Though not in darkness. Purple was the face
Of heav'n. Beneath my feet the valleys glow'd.
A range immense of wood-invested hills,
The boundaries of Greece, were clad in flames;
An act of froward chance, or crafty foes,
To cast dismay. The crackling pines I heard;
Their branches sparkled, and the thickets blaz'd.
In hillocks embers rose. Embody'd fire,
As from unnumber'd furnaces, I saw
Mount high, through vacant trunks of headless oaks,
Broad-bas'd, and dry with age. Barbarian helms,
Shields, javelins, sabres, gleaming from below,
Full soon discover'd to my tortur'd sight
The straits in Persia's pow'r. The Phocian chief,
Whate'er the cause, relinquishing his post,
Was to a neighb'ring eminence remov'd;
There, by the foe neglected or contemn'd,
Remain'd in arms, and neither fled nor fought.
I stay'd for day-spring; then the Persians mov'd.
To-morrow's sun will see their numbers here.'

He said no more. Unutterable fear
In horrid silence wraps the list'ning crowd,
Aghast, confounded. Silent are the chiefs,
Who feel no terror; yet, in wonder fix'd,
Thick-wedg'd, enclose Leonidas around,
Who thus in calmest elocution spake—

' I now behold the oracle fulfill'd.
Then art thou near, thou glorious, sacred hour,
Which shalt my country's liberty secure.
Thrice hail, thou solemn period! Thee the tongues
Of virtue, fame, and freedom, shall proclaim,
Shall celebrate, in ages yet unborn.
Thou godlike offspring of a godlike sire,
To him my kindest greetings, Medon, bear.
Farewell, Megistias, holy friend, and brave!
Thou too, experienc'd, venerable chief,
Demophilus, farewell! Farewell to thee,
Invincible Diomedon! to thee,
Unequall'd Dithyrambus! and to all,
Ye other dauntless warriors, who may claim
Praise from my lips, and friendship from my heart!
You, after all the wonders which your swords

Have here accomplish'd, will enrich your names
By fresh renown. Your valour must complete
What our's begins. Here first th' astonish'd foe
On dying Spartans shall, with terror, gaze
And tremble, while he conquers. Then, by fate
Led from his dreadful victory to meet
United Greece in phalanx o'er the plain,
By your avenging spears himself shall fall.'

  Forth from th' assembly strides Platæa's chief—
' By the twelve gods, enthron'd in heav'n supreme,
By my fair name, unsully'd yet, I swear
Thine eye, Leonidas, shall ne'er behold
Diomedon forsake thee. First let strength
Desert my limbs, and fortitude my heart.
Did I not face the Marathonian war?
Have I not seen Thermopylæ? What more
Can fame bestow, which I should wait to share?
Where can I, living, purchase brighter praise
Than dying here? What more illustrious tomb
Can I obtain than, bury'd in the heaps
Of Persians, fall'n my victims, on this rock
To lie, distinguish'd by a thousand wounds?'

He ended; when Demophilus—' O king
Of Lacedæmon, pride of human race,
Whom none e'er equall'd but the seed of Jove,
Thy own forefather, number'd with the gods,
Lo, I am old! With falt'ring steps I tread
The prone descent of years. My country claim'd
My youth, my ripeness. Feeble age but yields
An empty name of service. What remains
For me, unequal to the winged speed
Of active hours, which court the swift and young?
What eligible wish can wisdom form,
But to die well? Demophilus shall close
With thee, O hero, on this glorious earth
His eve of life.' The youth of Thespia next
Address'd Leonidas—' O first of Greeks,
Me too think worthy to attend thy fame
With this most dear, this venerable man,
For ever honour'd from my tend'rest age,
Ev'n till on life's extremity we part.
Nor too aspiring let my hopes be deem'd.
Should the Barbarian in his triumph mark
My youthful limbs among the gory heaps,
Perhaps remembrance may unnerve his arm

In future fields of contest with a race,
To whom the flow'r, the blooming joys, of life
Are less alluring than a noble death.'

To him his second parent—' Wilt thou bleed,
My Dithyrambus? But I here withhold
All counsel from thee, who art wise as brave.
I know thy magnanimity. I read
Thy gen'rous thoughts. Decided is thy choice.
Come then, attendants on a godlike shade,
When to th' Elysian ancestry of Greece
Descends her great protector, we will shew
To Harmatides an illustrious son,
And no unworthy brother. We will link
Our shields together. We will press the ground,
Still undivided in the arms of death.
So, if th' attentive traveller we draw
To our cold reliques, wond'ring, shall he trace
The diff'rent scene; then, pregnant with applause,
" O wise old man," exclaim, " the hour of fate
Well didst thou choose; and, O unequall'd youth,
Who for thy country didst thy bloom devote,
Mayst thou remain for ever dear to fame!

May time rejoice to name thee! O'er thy urn
May everlasting peace her pinion spread." '

This said, the hero with his lifted shield
His face o'ershades; he drops a secret tear:
Not this a tear of anguish, but deriv'd
From fond affection, grown mature with time,
Awak'd a manly tenderness alone,
Unmix'd with pity, or with vain regret.

A stream of duty, gratitude, and love,
Flow'd from the heart of Harmatides' son,
Addressing straight Leonidas, whose looks
Declar'd unspeakable applause—' O king
Of Lacedæmon, now distribute praise
From thy accustom'd justice, small to me,
To him a portion large. His guardian care,
His kind instruction, his example, train'd
My infancy, my youth. From him I learn'd
To live unspotted. Could I less than learn
From him to die with honour?' Medon hears.
Shook by a whirlwind of contending thoughts,
Strong heaves his manly bosom, under awe

Of wise Melissa, torn by friendship, fir'd
By such example high. In dubious state
So rolls a vessel, when th' inflated waves
Her planks assail, and winds her canvass rend;
The rudder labours, and requires a hand
Of firm, delib'rate skill. The gen'rous king
Perceives the hero's struggle, and prepares
To interpose relief; when instant came
Dieneces before them. Short he spake—

' Barbarian myriads through the secret pass
Have enter'd Greece. Leonidas, by morn
Expect them here. My slender force I spar'd.
There to have died was useless. We return
With thee to perish. Union of our strength
Will render more illustrious to ourselves,
And to the foe more terrible, our fall.'

Megistias last accosts Laconia's king—
' Thou, whom the gods have chosen to exalt
Above mankind in virtue and renown,
O call not me presumptuous, who implore
Among these heroes thy regardful ear.

To Lacedæmon I a stranger came,
There found protection. There to honours rais'd,
I have not yet the benefit repaid.
That now the gen'rous Spartans may behold
In me their large beneficence not vain,
Here to their cause I consecrate my breath.'

' Not so, Megistias,' interpos'd the king.
' Thou and thy son retire.' Again the seer—

' Forbid it, thou eternally ador'd,
O Jove, confirm my persevering soul!
Nor let me these auspicious moments lose,
When to my bounteous patrons I may shew
That I deserv'd their favour. Thou, my child,
Dear Menalippus, heed the king's command,
And my paternal tenderness revere.
Thou from these ranks withdraw thee, to my use
Thy arms surrend'ring. Fortune will supply
New proofs of valour. Vanquish then, or find
A glorious grave; but spare thy father's eye
The bitter anguish to behold thy youth
Untimely bleed before him.' Grief suspends

His speech, and interchangeably their arms
Impart the last embraces.   Either weeps,
The hoary parent and the blooming son.

But from his temples the pontific wreath
Megistias now unloosens.   He resigns
His hallow'd vestments; while the youth in tears
The helmet o'er his parent's snowy locks,
O'er his broad chest adjusts the radiant mail.

Dieneces was nigh.   Oppress'd by shame,
His downcast visage Menalippus hid
From him, who cheerful thus—' Thou needst not blush.
Thou hear'st thy father and the king command,
What I suggested, thy departure hence.
Train'd by my care, a soldier thou return'st.
Go, practise my instructions.   Oft in fields
Of future conflict may thy prowess call
Me to remembrance.   Spare thy words.   Farewell!'

While such contempt of life, such fervid zeal
To die with glory, animate the Greeks,
Far diff'rent thoughts possess Argestes' soul.

Amaze and mingled terror chill his blood.
Cold drops, distill'd from ev'ry pore, bedew
His shiv'ring flesh. His bosom pants. His knees
Yield to their burden. Ghastly pale his cheeks;
Pale are his lips, and trembling. Such the minds
Of slaves corrupt; on them the beauteous face
Of virtue turns to horror. But these words
From Lacedæmon's chief the wretch relieve—

' Return to Xerxes. Tell him, on this rock
The Grecians, faithful to their trust, await
His chosen myriads. Tell him, thou hast seen
How far the lust of empire is below
A freeborn spirit; that my death, which seals
My country's safety, is indeed a boon
His folly gives; a precious boon, which Greece
Will by perdition to his throne repay.'

He said. The Persian hastens through the pass.
Once more the stern Diomedon arose.
Wrath overcast his forehead while he spake—

' Yet more must stay and bleed. Detested Thebes

Ne'er shall receive her traitors back. This spot
Shall see their perfidy aton'd by death,
Ev'n from that pow'r to which their abject hearts
Have sacrific'd their faith. Nor dare to hope,
Ye vile deserters of the public weal,
Ye coward slaves, that, mingled in the heaps
Of gen'rous victims to their country's good,
You shall your shame conceal. Whoe'er shall pass
Along this field of glorious slain, and mark
For veneration ev'ry nobler corse,
His heart, though warm in rapturous applause,
Awhile shall curb the transport, to repeat
His execrations o'er such impious heads,
On whom that fate, to others yielding fame,
Is infamy and vengeance.' Dreadful thus
On the pale Thebans sentence he pronounc'd.
Like Rhadamanthus, from th' infernal seat
Of judgment, which inexorably dooms
The guilty dead to ever-during pain;
While Phlegethon his flaming volumes rolls
Before their sight, and ruthless furies shake
Their hissing serpents. All the Greeks assent
In clamours, echoing through the concave rock.

Forth Anaxander in th' assembly stood,
Which he address'd with indignation feign'd.

' If yet your clamours, Grecians, are allay'd,
Lo! I appear before you, to demand
Why these my brave companions, who alone
Among the Thebans, through dissuading crowds,
Their passage forc'd to join your camp, should bear
The name of traitors? By an exil'd wretch
We are traduc'd; by Demaratus, driv'n
From Spartan confines, who hath meanly sought
Barbarian courts for shelter. Hath he drawn
Such virtues thence, that Sparta, who before
Held him unworthy of his native sway,
Should trust him now, and doubt auxiliar friends?
Injurious man! We scorn the thoughts of flight.
Let Asia bring her numbers; unconstrain'd,
We will confront them, and for Greece expire.'

Thus in the garb of virtue he adorn'd
Necessity. Laconia's king perceiv'd,
Through all its fair disguise, the traitor's heart.
So, when at first mankind in science rude

Rever'd the moon, as bright in native beams,
Some sage, who walk'd with nature through her works,
By wisdom led, discern'd the various orb,
Dark in itself, in foreign splendours clad.

    Leonidas concludes—' Ye Spartans, hear;
Hear you, O Grecians, in our lot by choice
Partakers, destin'd to enroll your names
In time's eternal record, and enhance
Your country's lustre: lo! the noontide blaze
Inflames the broad horizon. Each retire;
Each in his tent invoke the pow'r of sleep,
To brace his vigour, to enlarge his strength
For long endurance. When the sun descends,
Let each appear in arms. You, brave allies
Of Corinth, Phlius, and Mycenæ's tow'rs,
Arcadians, Locrians, must not yet depart.
While we repose, embattled wait. Retreat
When we our tents abandon. I resign
To great Oïleus' son supreme command.
Take my embraces, Æschylus. The fleet
Expects thee. To Themistocles report
What thou hast seen and heard.' ' O thrice farewell!'

Th' Athenian answer'd—' To yourselves, my friends,
Your virtues immortality secure,
Your bright examples victory to Greece.'

    Retaining these injunctions, all dispers'd;
While in his tent Leonidas remain'd
Apart with Agis, whom he thus bespake—
' Yet in our fall the pond'rous hand of Greece
Shall Asia feel. This Persian's welcome tale
Of us, inextricably doom'd her prey,
As by the force of sorcery, will wrap
Security around her, will suppress
All sense, all thought, of danger. Brother, know
That, soon as Cynthia from the vault of heav'n
Withdraws her shining lamp, through Asia's host
Shall massacre and desolation rage.
Yet not to base associates will I trust
My vast design. Their perfidy might warn
The unsuspecting foe, our fairest fruits
Of glory thus be wither'd. Ere we move,
While, on the solemn sacrifice intent,
As Lacedæmon's ancient laws ordain,
Our pray'rs we offer to the tuneful nine,

Thou whisper, through the willing ranks of Thebes,
Slow, and in silence, to disperse and fly.'

Now, left by Agis, on his couch reclin'd,
The Spartan king thus meditates alone—

' My fate is now impending. O my soul,
What more auspicious period couldst thou choose
For death than now, when, beating high in joy,
Thou tell'st me I am happy? If to live,
Or die, as virtue dictates, be to know
The purest bliss; if she her charms displays,
Still lovely, still unfading, still serene,
To youth, to age, to death; whatever be
Those other climes of happiness unchang'd,
Which heav'n in dark futurity conceals,
Still here, O virtue, thou art all our good.
Oh! what a black, unspeakable reverse
Must the unrighteous, must the tyrant prove?
What in the struggle of departing day,
When life's last glimpse, extinguishing, presents
Unknown, inextricable gloom? But how
Can I explain the terrors of a breast

Where guilt resides? Leonidas, forego
The horrible conception, and again
Within thy own felicity retire;
Bow grateful down to him, who form'd thy mind
Of crimes unfruitful, never to admit
The black impression of a guilty thought.
Else could I fearless, by delib'rate choice,
Relinquish life? This calm from minds deprav'd
Is ever absent. Oft in them the force
Of some prevailing passion for a time
Suppresses fear. Precipitate they lose
The sense of danger; when dominion, wealth,
Or purple pomp, enchant the dazzled sight,
Pursuing still the joys of life alone.
But he, who calmly seeks a certain death,
When duty only, and the gen'ral good,
Direct his courage, must a soul possess,
Which, all content deducing from itself,
Can, by unerring virtue's constant light,
Discern when death is worthy of his choice.
The man, thus great and happy, in the scope
Of his large mind is stretch'd beyond his date.
Ev'n on this shore of being he in thought,

Supremely bless'd, anticipates the good,
Which late posterity from him derives.'

At length the hero's meditations close.
The swelling transport of his heart subsides
In soft oblivion; and the silken plumes
Of sleep envelope his extended limbs.

LEONIDAS.

BOOK XI.

THE ARGUMENT.

Leonidas, rising before sun-set, dismisses the forces under the command of Medon; but, observing a reluctance in him to depart, reminds him of his duty, and gives him an affectionate farewell. He then relates to his own select band a dream, which is interpreted by Megistias; arms himself, and marches, in procession with his whole troop, to an altar newly raised on a neighbouring meadow; there offers a sacrifice to the muses: he invokes the assistance of those goddesses; he animates his companions; then, placing himself at their head, leads them against the enemy in the dead of the night.

LEONIDAS.

BOOK XI.

The day was closing. Agis left his tent.
He sought his godlike brother. Him he found
Stretch'd o'er his tranquil couch. His looks retain'd
The cheerful tincture of his waking thoughts,
To gladden sleep. So smile soft ev'ning skies,
Yet streak'd with ruddy light, when summer's suns
Have veil'd their beaming foreheads. Transport fill'd
The eye of Agis; friendship swell'd his heart;
His yielding knee in veneration bent;
The hero's hand he kiss'd, then fervent thus—

'O excellence ineffable, receive
This secret homage; and may gentle sleep
Yet longer seal thine eyelids, that, unblam'd,
I may fall down before thee.' He concludes

In adoration of his friend divine,
Whose brow the shades of slumber now forsake.
So, when the rising sun resumes his state,
Some white-rob'd magus on Euphrates' side,
Or Indian seer on Ganges, prostrate falls
Before th' emerging glory, to salute
That radiant emblem of th' immortal mind.

    Uprise both heroes. From their tents in arms
Appear the bands elect. The other Greeks
Are filing homeward. Only Medon stops.
Melissa's dictates he forgets awhile.
All inattentive to the warning voice
Of Melibœus, earnest he surveys
Leonidas. Such constancy of zeal
In good Oïleus' offspring brings the sire
To full remembrance in that solemn hour,
And draws these cordial accents from the king—

    ' Approach me, Locrian. In thy look I trace
Consummate faith and love. But, vers'd in arms,
Against thy gen'ral's orders wouldst thou stay?
Go, prove to kind Oïleus that my heart

Of him was mindful when the gates of death
I barr'd against his son. Yon gallant Greeks,
To thy commanding care from mine transfer'd,
Remove from certain slaughter. Last repair
To Lacedæmon. Thither lead thy sire.
Say to her senate, to her people tell,
Here didst thou leave their countrymen and king,
On death resolv'd, obedient to the laws.'

' The Locrian chief, restraining tears, replies—
' My sire, left slumb'ring in the island-fane,
Awoke no more.' ' Then joyful I shall meet
Him soon,' the king made answer. ' Let thy worth
Supply thy father's. Virtue bids me die,
Thee live. Farewell.' Now Medon's grief, o'er-aw'd
By wisdom, leaves his long-suspended mind
To firm decision. He departs, prepar'd
For all the duties of a man, by deeds
To prove himself the friend of Sparta's king,
Melissa's brother, and Oïleus' son.

The gen'rous victims of the public weal,
Assembled now, Leonidas salutes,

His pregnant soul disburd'ning—' O, thrice hail!
Surround me, Grecians; to my words attend.—
This evening's sleep no sooner press'd my brows,
Than o'er my head the empyreal form
Of heav'n-enthron'd Alcides was display'd.
I saw his magnitude divine. His voice
I heard, his solemn mandate to arise.
I rose. He bade me follow. I obey'd.
A mountain's summit, clear'd from mist or cloud,
We reach'd in silence. Suddenly the howl
Of wolves and dogs, the vulture's piercing shriek,
The yell of ev'ry beast and bird of prey,
Discordant grated on my ear. I turn'd.
A surface hideous, delug'd o'er with blood,
Beyond my view illimitably stretch'd,
One vast expanse of horror. There, supine,
Of huge dimension, cov'ring half the plain,
A giant corse lay mangled, red with wounds,
Delv'd in th' enormous flesh, which, bubbling, fed
Ten thousand thousand grisly beaks and jaws,
Insatiably devouring. Mute I gaz'd;
When from behind I heard a second sound,
Like surges tumbling o'er a craggy shore.

Again I turn'd. An ocean there appear'd
With riven keels and shrouds, with shiver'd oars,
With arms and welt'ring carcasses bestrewn,
Innumerous. The billows foam'd in blood.
But where the waters, unobserv'd before,
Between two adverse shores, contracting roll'd
A stormy current, on the beach forlorn
One of majestic stature I descry'd,
In ornaments imperial. Oft he bent
On me his clouded eyeballs. Oft my name
He sounded forth in execrations loud;
Then rent his splendid garments; then his head
In rage divested of its graceful hairs.
Impatient now he ey'd a slender skiff,
Which, mounted high on boist'rous waves, approach'd.
With indignation, with reluctant grief,
Once more his sight reverting, he embark'd
Amid the perils of the frowning deep.
" O thou, by glorious actions rank'd in heav'n,"
I here exclaim'd, " instruct me. What produc'd
This desolation?" Hercules reply'd;
" Let thy astonish'd eye again survey
The scene thy soul abhorr'd." I look'd. I saw

A land where plenty, with disporting hands,
Pour'd all the fruits of Amalthea's horn;
Where bloom'd the olive; where the clust'ring vine
With her broad foliage mantled ev'ry hill;
Where Ceres with exuberance enrob'd
The pregnant bosoms of the fields in gold;
Where spacious towns, whose circuits proud contain'd
The dazzling works of wealth, along the banks
Of copious rivers shew'd their stately tow'rs,
The strength and splendour of the peopled land.
Then in a moment clouds obscur'd my view;
At once all vanish'd from my waking eyes.'

'Thrice I salute the omen,' loud began
The sage Megistias. 'In this mystic dream
I see my country's victories. The land,
The deep, shall own her triumphs; while the tears
Of Asia and of Libya shall deplore
Their offspring, cast before the vulture's beak,
And ev'ry monstrous native of the main.
These joyous fields of plenty picture Greece,
Enrich'd by conquest and Barbarian spoils.
He, whom thou saw'st, in regal vesture clad,

Print on the sand his solitary step,
Is Xerxes, foil'd and fugitive.' So spake
The rev'rend augur. Ev'ry bosom felt
Enthusiastic rapture, joy beyond
All sense and all conception, but of those
Who die to save their country. Here again
Th' exulting band Leonidas address'd—

' Since happiness from virtue is deriv'd,
Who for his country dies, that moment proves
Most happy, as most virtuous. Such our lot.
But go, Megistias; instantly prepare
The sacred fuel, and the victim due,
That to the muses (so by Sparta's law
We are enjoin'd) our off'rings may be paid
Before we march. Remember, from the rites
Let ev'ry sound be absent; not the fife,
Not ev'n the music-breathing flute, be heard.
Meantime, ye leaders, ev'ry band instruct
To move in silence.' Mindful of their charge,
The chiefs depart. Leonidas provides
His various armour. Agis close attends,
His best assistant. First a breastplate arms

The spacious chest.   O'er this the hero spreads
The mailed cuirass, from his shoulders hung.
A shining belt infolds his mighty loins.
Next, on his stately temples he erects
The plumed helm; then grasps his pond'rous shield;
Where, nigh the centre, on projecting brass,
Th' inimitable artist had emboss'd
The shape of great Alcides, whom to gain
Two goddesses contended.   Pleasure here
Won, by soft wiles, th' attracted eye; and there
The form of Virtue dignify'd the scene.
In her majestic sweetness was display'd
The mind sublime and happy.   From her lips
Seem'd eloquence to flow.   In look serene,
But fix'd intensely on the son of Jove,
She wav'd her hand, where, winding to the skies,
Her paths ascended.   On the summit stood,
Supported by a trophy near to heav'n,
Fame, and protended her eternal trump.
The youth, attentive to her wisdom, own'd
The prevalence of Virtue; while his eye,
Fill'd by that spirit which redeem'd the world
From tyranny and monsters, darted flames,

Not undescry'd by Pleasure, where she lay
Beneath a gorgeous canopy.   Around
Were flow'rets strewn, and wantonly in rills
A fount meander'd.   All relax'd her limbs;
Nor wanting yet solicitude to gain,
What lost she fear'd, as struggling with despair,
She seem'd collecting ev'ry pow'r to charm:
Excess of sweet allurement she diffus'd
In vain.   Still Virtue sway'd Alcides' mind.
Hence all his labours.   Wrought with vary'd art,
The shield's external surface they enrich'd.

   This portraiture of glory on his arm
Leonidas displays, and, tow'ring, strides
From his pavilion.   Ready are the bands.
The chiefs assume their station.   Torches blaze
Through ev'ry file.   All now in silent pace
To join in solemn sacrifice proceed.
First Polydorus bears the hallow'd knife,
The sacred salt and barley.   At his side
Diomedon sustains a weighty mace.
The priest, Megistias, follows like the rest
In polish'd armour.   White as winter's fleece,

A fillet round his shining helm reveals
The sacerdotal honours. By the horns,
Where laurels twine, with Alpheus, Maron leads
The consecrated ox. And lo! behind
Leonidas advances. Never he
In such transcendent majesty was seen,
And his own virtue never so enjoy'd.
Successive move Dieneces the brave;
In hoary state Demophilus; the bloom
Of Dithyrambus, glowing in the hope
Of future praise; the gen'rous Agis next,
Serene and graceful; last the Theban chiefs,
Repining, ignominious; then slow march
The troops, all mute, nor shake their brazen arms.

Not from Thermopylæ remote the hills
Of Oeta, yielding to a fruitful dale,
Within their side, half-circling, had enclos'd
A fair expanse in verdure smooth. The bounds
Were edg'd by wood, o'erlook'd by snowy cliffs,
Which from the clouds bent, frowning. Down a rock,
Above the loftiest summit of the grove,
A tumbling torrent wore the shagged stone;

Then, gleaming through the intervals of shade,
Attain'd the valley, where the level stream
Diffus'd refreshment. On its banks the Greeks
Had rais'd a rustic altar, fram'd of turf.
Broad was the surface, high in piles of wood,
All interspers'd with laurel. Purer deem'd
Than river, lake, or fountain, in a vase
Old Ocean's briny element was plac'd
Before the altar; and of wine unmix'd
Capacious goblets stood. Megistias now
His helm unloosen'd. With his snowy head
Uncover'd, round the solemn pile he trod.
He shook a branch of laurel, scatt'ring wide
The sacred moisture of the main. His hand
Next on the altar, on the victim strew'd
The mingled salt and barley. O'er the horns
Th' inverted chalice, foaming from the grape,
Discharg'd a rich libation. Then approach'd
Diomedon. Megistias gave the sign.
Down sunk the victim by a deathful stroke,
Nor groan'd. The augur bury'd in the throat
His hallow'd steel. A purple current flow'd.
Now smok'd the structure, now it flam'd abroad

In sudden splendour. Deep in circling ranks
The Grecians press'd. Each held a sparkling brand;
The beaming lances intermix'd; the helms,
The burnish'd armour, multiply'd the blaze.
Leonidas drew nigh. Before the pile
His feet he planted. From his brows remov'd,
The casque to Agis he consign'd; his shield,
His spear, to Dithyrambus; then, his arms
Extending, forth in supplication broke—

' Harmonious daughters of Olympian Jove,
Who, on the top of Helicon ador'd,
And high Parnassus, with delighted ears
Bend to the warble of Castalia's stream,
Or Aganippe's murmur, if from thence
We must invoke your presence, or along
The neighb'ring mountains with propitious steps
If now you grace your consecrated bow'rs,
Look down, ye Muses; nor disdain to stand
Each an immortal witness of our fate.
But with you bring fair Liberty, whom Jove
And you must honour. Let her sacred eyes
Approve her dying Grecians; let her voice

In exultation tell the earth and heav'ns
These are her sons.   Then strike your tuneful shells.
Record us guardians of our parent's age,
Our matron's virtue, and our children's bloom,
The glorious bulwarks of our country's laws,
Who shall ennoble the historian's page,
Shall on the joyous festival inspire
With loftier strains the virgin's choral song.
Then, O celestial maids, on yonder camp
Let night sit heavy.   Let a sleep like death
Weigh down the eye of Asia.   O infuse
A cool, untroubled spirit in our breasts,
Which may in silence guide our daring feet,
Controul our fury, nor by tumult wild
The friendly dark affright, till dying groans
Of slaughter'd tyrants into horror wake
The midnight calm; then turn destruction loose.
Let terror, let confusion, rage around;
In one vast ruin heap the barb'rous ranks,
Their horse, their chariots.   Let the spurning steed
Imbrue his hoofs in blood, the shatter'd cars
Crush with their brazen weight the prostrate necks
Of chiefs and kings, encircled, as they fall,

By nations slain. You, countrymen and friends,
My last commands retain. Your gen'ral's voice
Once more salutes you, not to rouse the brave,
Or minds resolv'd and dauntless to confirm.
Too well by this expiring blaze I see
Impatient valour flash from ev'ry eye.
O temper well that ardour, and your lips
Close on the rising transport. Mark how sleep
Hath folded millions in his black embrace.
No sound is wafted from th' unnumber'd foe.
The winds themselves are silent. All conspires
To this great sacrifice, where thousands soon
Shall only wake to die. Their crowded train
This night perhaps to Pluto's dreary shades
Ev'n Xerxes' ghost may lead, unless reserv'd
From this destruction to lament a doom
Of more disgrace, when Greece confounds that pow'r
Which we will shake. But look, the setting moon
Shuts on our darksome paths her waining horns.
Let each his head distinguish by a wreath
Of well-earn'd laurel. Then the victim share,
Then crown the goblet. Take your last repast;

With your forefathers, and the heroes old
You next will banquet in the bless'd abodes.'

  Here ends their leader. Through th' encircling
   crowd
The agitation of their spears denotes
High ardour. So the spiry growth of pines
Is rock'd, when Æolus in eddies winds
Among their stately trunks on Pelion's brow.
The Acarnanian seer distributes swift
The sacred laurel. Snatch'd in eager zeal,
Around each helm the woven leaves unite
Their glossy verdure to the floating plumes.
Then is the victim portion'd. In the bowl
Then flows the vine's empurpled stream. Aloof
The Theban train, in wan dejection mute,
Brood o'er their shame, or cast affrighted looks
On that determin'd courage which, unmov'd
At fate's approach, with cheerful lips could taste
The sparkling goblet, could in joy partake
That last, that glorious banquet. Ev'n the heart
Of Anaxander had forgot its wiles,
Dissembling fear no longer. Agis here,

Regardful ever of the king's command,
Accosts the Theban chiefs in whispers thus—

' Leonidas permits you to retire.
While on the rites of sacrifice employ'd,
None heed your motions. Separate, and fly
In silent pace.' This heard, th' inglorious troop,
Their files dissolving, from the rest withdraw.
Unseen they moulder from the host, like snow,
Freed from the rigour of constraining frost;
Soon as the sun exerts his orient beam,
The transitory landscape melts in rills
Away; and structures, which delude the eye,
Insensibly are lost. The solemn feast
Was now concluded. Now Laconia's king
Had reassum'd his arms. Before his step
The crowd roll backward. In their gladden'd sight
His crest, illumin'd by uplifted brands,
Its purple splendour shakes. The tow'ring oak
Thus from a lofty promontory waves
His majesty of verdure. As with joy
The sailors mark his heav'n-ascending pride,
Which from afar directs their foamy course

Along the pathless ocean; so the Greeks
In transport gaze, as down their op'ning ranks
The king proceeds; from whose superior frame
A soul like thine, O Phidias, might conceive,
In Parian marble or effulgent brass,
The form of great Apollo; when the god,
Won by the pray'rs of man's afflicted race,
In arms forsook his lucid throne, to pierce
The monster Python in the Delphian vale.
Close by the hero Polydorus waits,
To guide destruction through the Asian tents.
As the young eagle near his parent's side
In wanton flight essays his vig'rous wing,
Ere long with her to penetrate the clouds,
To dart impetuous on the fleecy train,
And dye his beak in gore; by Sparta's king
The injur'd Polydorus thus prepares
His arm for death. He feasts his angry soul
On promis'd vengeance. His impatient thoughts
Ev'n now transport him furious to the seat
Of his long sorrows, not with fetter'd hands,
But now once more a Spartan, with his spear,
His shield, restor'd, to lead his country's bands,

And with them devastation. Nor the rest
Neglect to form. Thick-rang'd, the helmets blend
Their various plumes, as intermingling oaks
Combine their foliage in Dodona's grove;
Or as the cedars on the Syrian hills
Their shady texture spread. Once more the king,
O'er all the phalanx his consid'rate view
Extending, through the ruddy gleam descries
One face of gladness; but the godlike van
He most contemplates: Agis, Alpheus there,
Megistias, Maron, with Platæa's chief,
Dieneces, Demophilus, are seen
With Thespia's youth: nor they their steady sight
From his remove, in speechless transport bound
By love, by veneration, till they hear
His last injunction. To their diff'rent posts
They sep'rate. Instant on the dewy turf
Are cast th' extinguish'd brands. On all around
Drops sudden darkness; on the wood, the hill,
The snowy ridge, the vale, the silver stream.
It verg'd on midnight. Tow'rd the hostile camp,
In march compos'd and silent, down the pass
The phalanx mov'd. Each patient bosom hush'd

Its struggling spirit, nor in whispers breath'd
The rapt'rous ardour virtue then inspir'd.
So low'ring clouds along th' ethereal void,
In slow expansion, from the gloomy north
Awhile suspend their horrors, destin'd soon
To blaze in lightnings, and to burst in storms.

LEONIDAS.

BOOK XII.

THE ARGUMENT.

Leonidas and the Grecians penetrate through the Persian camp to the very pavilion of Xerxes, who avoids destruction by flight. The Barbarians are slaughtered in great multitudes, and their camp is set on fire. Leonidas conducts his men in good order back to Thermopylæ; engages the Persians who were descended from the hills; and, after numberless proofs of superior strength and valour, sinks down covered with wounds, and expires the last of all the Grecian commanders.

LEONIDAS.

BOOK XII.

Across th' unguarded bound of Asia's camp
Slow pass the Grecians. Through innum'rous tents,
Where all is mute and tranquil, they pursue
Their march sedate. Beneath the leaden hand
Of sleep lie millions motionless and deaf,
Nor dream of fate's approach. Their wary foes,
By Polydorus guided, still proceed.
Ev'n to the centre of th' extensive host
They pierce unseen; when lo! th' imperial tent
Yet distant rose before them. Spreading round
Th' august pavilion, was an ample space
For thousands in arrangement. Here a band
Of chosen Persians, watchful o'er the king,
Held their nocturnal station. As the hearts
Of anxious nations, whom th' unsparing sword

Or famine threaten, tremble at the sight
Of fear-engender'd phantoms in the sky,
Aerial hosts amid the clouds array'd,
Portending wo and death; the Persian guard
In equal consternation now descry'd
The glimpse of hostile armour. All disband,
As if auxiliar to his favour'd Greeks
Pan held their banner, scatt'ring from its folds
Fear and confusion, which to Xerxes' couch,
Swift-winged, fly; thence shake the gen'ral camp,
Whose numbers issue naked, pale, unarm'd,
Wild in amazement, blinded by dismay,
To ev'ry foe obnoxious. In the breasts
Of thousands, gor'd at once, the Grecian steel
Reeks in destruction. Deluges of blood
Float o'er the field, and foam around the heaps
Of wretches slain, unconscious of the hand
Which wastes their helpless multitude. Amaze,
Affright, distraction, from his pillow chase
The lord of Asia, who in thought beholds
United Greece in arms. Thy lust of pow'r!
Thy hope of glory! whither are they flown,
With all thy pomp? In this disast'rous hour

What could avail th' immeasurable range
Of thy proud camp, save only to conceal
Thy trembling steps, O Xerxes, while thou fly'st?
To thy deserted couch, with other looks,
With other steps, Leonidas is nigh.
Before him terror strides. Gigantic death.
And desolation at his side attend.

The vast pavilion's empty space, where lamps
Of gold shed light and odours, now admits
The hero. Ardent throngs behind him press,
But miss their victim. To the ground are hurl'd
The glitt'ring ensigns of imperial state.
The diadem, the sceptre, late ador'd
Through boundless kingdoms, underneath their feet,
In mingled rage and scorn, the warriors crush,
A sacrifice to freedom. They return
Again to form. Leonidas exalts
For new destruction his resistless spear;
When double darkness suddenly descends.
The clouds, condensing, intercept the stars.
Black o'er the furrow'd main the raging east
In whirlwinds sweeps the surge. The coasts resound.

The cavern'd rocks, the crashing forests, roar.
Swift through the camp the hurricane impels
Its rude career; when Asia's numbers, veil'd
Amid the shelt'ring horrors of the storm,
Evade the victor's lance. The Grecians halt;
While to their gen'ral's pregnant mind occurs
A new attempt and vast. Perpetual fire
Beside the tent of Xerxes, from the hour
He lodg'd his standards on the Malian plains,
Had shone. Among his Magi, to adore
Great Horomazes was the monarch wont
Before the sacred light. Huge piles of wood
Lay nigh, prepar'd to feed the constant flame.
On living embers these are cast. So wills
Leonidas. The phalanx then divides.
Four troops are form'd, by Dithyrambus led,
By Alpheus, by Diomedon. The last .
Himself conducts. The word is giv'n. They seize
The burning fuel. Sparkling in the wind,
Destructive fire is brandish'd. All, enjoin'd
To reassemble at the regal tent,
By various paths the hostile camp invade.

Now devastation, unconfin'd, involves

The Malian fields. Among Barbarian tents,
From diff'rent stations, fly consuming flames.
The Greeks afford no respite; and the storm
Exasperates the blaze. To ev'ry part
The conflagration like a sea expands,
One waving surface of unbounded fire.
In ruddy volumes mount the curling flames
To heav'n's dark vault, and paint the midnight clouds.
So, when the north emits his purpled lights,
The undulated radiance, streaming wide,
As with a burning canopy, invests
Th' ethereal concave. Oeta now disclos'd
His forehead, glitt'ring in eternal frost,
While down his rocks the foamy torrents shone.
Far o'er the main the pointed rays were thrown;
Night snatch'd her mantle from the ocean's breast;
The billows glimmer'd from the distant shores.

But lo! a pillar huge of smoke ascends,
Which overshades the field. There horror, there
Leonidas, presides. Command he gave
To Polydorus, who, exulting, shew'd
Where Asia's horse and warlike cars possess'd

A crowded station. At the hero's nod
Devouring Vulcan riots on the stores
Of Ceres, empty'd of the ripen'd grain,
On all the tribute from her meadows brown,
By rich Thessalia render'd to the scythe.
A flood of fire envelopes all the ground.
The cordage bursts around the blazing tents.
Down sink the roofs on suffocated throngs,
Close-wedg'd by fear. The Libyan chariot burns.
Th' Arabian camel and the Persian steed
Bound through a burning deluge. Wild with pain,
They shake their singed manes. Their madding hoofs
Dash through the blood of thousands, mix'd with flames,
Which rage, augmented by the whirlwind's blast.

 Meantime the sceptred lord of half the globe
From tent to tent precipitates his flight.
Dispers'd are all his satraps. Pride herself
Shuns his dejected brow. Despair alone
Waits on th' imperial fugitive, and shews,
As round the camp his eye, distracted, roves,
No limits to destruction. Now is seen
Aurora, mounting from her eastern hill

In rosy sandals, and with dewy locks.
The winds subside before her; darkness flies;
A stream of light proclaims the cheerful day,
Which sees at Xerxes' tent the conqu'ring bands,
All reunited. What could fortune more
To aid the valiant, what to gorge revenge?
Lo! desolation o'er the adverse host
Hath empty'd all her terrors. Ev'n the hand
Of languid slaughter dropt the crimson steel;
Nor nature longer can sustain the toil
Of unremitted conquest. Yet what pow'r
Among these sons of Liberty reviv'd
Their drooping warmth, new-strung their nerves, recall'd
Their weary'd swords to deeds of brighter fame?
What, but th' inspiring hope of glorious death
To crown their labours, and th' auspicious look
Of their heroic chief, which, still unchang'd,
Still in superior majesty, declar'd
No toil had yet relax'd his matchless strength,
Nor worn the vigour of his godlike soul.

Back to the pass, in gentle march, he leads
Th' embattled warriors. They behind the shrubs,

Where Medon sent such numbers to the shades,
In ambush lie. The tempest is o'erblown.
Soft breezes only from the Malian wave
O'er each grim face, besmear'd with smoke and gore,
Their cool refreshment breathe. The healing gale,
A crystal rill near Oeta's verdant feet,
Dispel the languor from their harass'd nerves,
Fresh brac'd by strength returning   O'er their heads
Lo! in full blaze of majesty appears
Melissa, bearing in her hand divine
Th' eternal guardian of illustrious deeds,
The sweet Phœbean lyre. Her graceful train
Of white-rob'd virgins, seated on a range
Half down the cliff, o'ershadowing the Greeks,
All with concordant strings and accents clear,
A torrent pour of melody, and swell
A high, triumphal, solemn, dirge of praise,
Anticipating fame. Of endless joys
In bless'd Elysium was the song—' Go, meet
Lycurgus, Solon, and Zaleucus sage,
Let them salute the children of their laws.
Meet Homer, Orpheus, and th' Ascræan bard,
Who, with a spirit by ambrosial food

Refin'd and more exalted, shall contend
Your splendid fate to warble through the bow'rs
Of amaranth and myrtle, ever young,
Like your renown. Your ashes we will cull.
In yonder fane deposited, your urns,
Dear to the Muses, shall our lays inspire.
Whatever off'rings genius, science, art,
Can dedicate to virtue, shall be yours,
The gifts of all the Muses, to transmit
You on th' enliven'd canvass, marble, brass,
In wisdom's volume, in the poet's song,
In ev'ry tongue, through ev'ry age and clime;
You of this earth the brightest flow'rs, not cropt,
Transplanted only to immortal bloom
Of praise with men, of happiness with gods.'

The Grecian valour on religion's flame
To ecstasy is wafted. Death is nigh.
As by the Graces fashion'd, he appears
A beauteous form. His adamantine gate
Is half unfolded. All in transport catch
A glimpse of immortality. Elate
In rapturous delusion, they believe

That to behold and solemnize their fate
The goddesses are present on the hills
With celebrating lyres. In thought serene
Leonidas the kind deception bless'd,
Nor undeceiv'd his soldiers. After all
Th' incessant labours of the horrid night,
Through blood, through flames, continu'd, he prepares
In order'd battle to confront the pow'rs
Of Hyperanthes from the upper straits.

Not long the Greeks in expectation wait
Impatient. Sudden, with tumultuous shouts,
Like Nile's rude current, where, in deaf'ning roar,
Prone from the steep of Elephantis, falls
A sea of waters, Hyperanthes pours
His chosen numbers on the Grecian camp
Down from the hills precipitant. No foes
He finds. The Thebans join him. In his van
They march conductors. On the Persians roll,
In martial thunder, through the sounding pass.
They issue forth, impetuous, from its mouth.
That moment Sparta's leader gave the sign;
When, as th' impulsive ram in forceful sway

O'erturns a nodding rampart from its base,
And strews a town with ruin, so the band
Of serry'd heroes down the Malian steep,
Tremendous depth, the mix'd battalions swept
Of Thebes and Persia. There no waters flow'd.
Abrupt and naked, all was rock beneath.
Leonidas, incens'd, with grappling strength
Dash'd Anaxander on a pointed crag;
Compos'd, then gave new orders. At the word
His phalanx, wheeling, penetrates the pass.
Astonish'd Persia stops in full career.
Ev'n Hyperanthes shrinks in wonder back.
Confusion drives fresh numbers from the shore.
The Malian ooze o'erwhelms them. Sparta's king
Still presses forward, till an open breadth
Of fifty paces yields his front extent
To proffer battle. Hyperanthes soon
Recalls his warriors, dissipates their fears.
Swift on the great Leonidas a cloud
Of darts is show'r'd. Th' encount'ring armies close.

Who first, sublimest hero, felt thy arm?
What rivers heard along their echoing banks

Thy name, in curses sounded from the lips
Of noble mothers, wailing for their sons?
What towns with empty monuments were fill'd
For those whom thy unconquerable sword
This day to vultures cast? First Bessus died,
A haughty satrap, whose tyrannic sway
Despoil'd Hyrcania of her golden sheaves,
And laid her forests waste. For him the bees
Among the branches interwove their sweets;
For him the fig was ripen'd, and the vine
In rich profusion o'er the goblet foam'd.
Then Dinis bled. On Hermus' side he reign'd;
He long, assiduous, unavailing, woo'd
The martial queen of Caria. She disdain'd
A lover's soft complaint. Her rigid ear
Was fram'd to watch the tempest while it rag'd,
Her eye accustom'd on the rolling deck
To brave the turgid billow. Near the shore
She now is present in her pinnace light,
The spectacle of glory crowds her breast
With diff'rent passions. Valiant, she applauds
The Grecian valour; faithful, she laments
Her sad presage of Persia; prompts her son

To emulation of the Greeks in arms,
And of herself in loyalty. By fate
Is she reserv'd to signalize that day
Of future shame, when Xerxes must behold
The blood of nations overflow his decks,
And to their bottom tinge the briny floods
Of Salamis; whence she with Asia flies,
She only not inglorious. Low reclines
Her lover now, on Hermus to repeat
Her name no more, nor tell the vocal groves
His fruitless sorrows. Next Maduces fell,
A Paphlagonian. Born amid the sound
Of chafing surges, and the roar of winds,
He o'er th' inhospitable Euxine foam
Was wont, from high Carambis' rock, to ken
Ill-fated keels, which cut the Pontic stream;
Then, with his dire associates, through the deep
For spoil and slaughter guide his savage prow.
Him dogs will rend ashore. From Medus far,
Their native current, two bold brothers died,
Sisamnes and Tithraustes, potent lords
Of rich domains. On these Mithrines grey,
Cilician prince, Lilæus, who had left

The balmy fragrance of Arabia's fields,
With Babylonian Tenagon, expir'd.

The growing carnage Hyperanthes views
Indignant, fierce in vengeful ardour strides
Against the victor. Each his lance protends.
But Asia's numbers interpose their shields,
Solicitous to guard a prince rever'd:
Or thither fortune whelm'd the tide of war,
His term protracting for augmented fame.
So two proud vessels, lab'ring on the foam,
Present for battle their destructive beaks;
When ridgy seas, by hurricanes uptorn,
In mountainous commotion dash between,
And either deck, in black'ning tempests veil'd,
Waft from its distant foe. More fiercely burn'd
Thy spirit, mighty Spartan. Such dismay
Relax'd thy foes, that each Barbarian heart
Resign'd all hopes of victory. The steeds
Of day were climbing their meridian height.
Continu'd shouts of onset from the pass
Resounded o'er the plain. Artuchus heard.
When first the spreading tumult had alarm'd

His distant quarter, starting from repose,
He down the valley of Spercheos rush'd,
To aid his regal master. Asia's camp
He found the seat of terror and despair.
As in some fruitful clime, which late hath known
The rage of winds and floods, although the storm
Be heard no longer, and the deluge fled,
Still o'er the wasted region nature mourns
In melancholy silence; through the grove
With prostrate glories lie the stately oak,
Th' uprooted elm and beach; the plain is spread
With fragments, swept from villages o'erthrown;
Around the pastures, flocks, and herds are cast
In dreary piles of death: so Persia's host,
In terror mute, one boundless scene displays
Of devastation. Half-devour'd by fire,
Her tall pavilions and her martial cars
Deform the wide encampment. Here in gore
Her princes welter, nameless thousands there,
Not victims all to Greeks. In gasping heaps
Barbarians, mangled by Barbarians, shew'd
The wild confusion of that direful night,
When, wanting signals, and a leader's care,

They rush'd on mutual slaughter. Xerxes' tent
On its exalted summit, when the dawn
First streak'd the orient sky, was wont to bear
The golden form of Mithra, clos'd between
Two lucid crystals. This the gen'ral host
Observ'd, their awful signal to arrange
In arms complete, and numberless to watch
Their monarch's rising. This conspicuous blaze
Artuchus places in th' accustom'd seat.
As, after winds have ruffled by a storm
The plumes of darkness, when her welcome face
The morning lifts serene, each wary swain
Collects his flock dispers'd; the neighing steed,
The herds forsake their shelter; all return
To well-known pastures, and frequented streams:
So now this cheering signal on the tent
Revives each leader. From inglorious flight
Their scatter'd bands they call, their wonted ground
Resume, and hail Artuchus. From their swarms
A force he culls. Thermopylæ he seeks.
Fell shouts in horrid dissonance precede.

    His phalanx swift Leonidas commands

To circle backward from the Malian bay.
Their order changes. Now, half-orb'd, they stand
By Oeta's fence protected from behind,
With either flank united to the rock.
As by th' excelling architect dispos'd
To shield some haven, a stupendous mole,
Fram'd of the grove and quarry's mingled strength,
In ocean's bosom penetrates afar:
There, pride of art, immovable it looks
On Eolus and Neptune; there defies
Those potent gods combin'd: unyielding thus,
The Grecians stood a solid mass of war
Against Artuchus, join'd with numbers new
To Hyperanthes. In the foremost rank
Leonidas his dreadful station held.
Around him soon a spacious void was seen,
By flight or slaughter in the Persian van.
In gen'rous shame and wrath Artuchus burns,
Discharging full at Lacedæmon's chief
An iron-studded mace. It glanc'd aside,
Turn'd by the massy buckler. Prone to earth
The satrap fell. Alcander aim'd his point,
Which had transfix'd him prostrate on the rock,

But for th' immediate succour he obtain'd
From faithful soldiers, lifting on their shields
A chief belov'd.   Not such Alcander's lot.
An arrow wounds his heart.   Supine he lies,
The on'y Theban who to Greece preserv'd
Unviolated faith.   Physician sage,
On pure Cithæron healing herbs to cull
Was he accustom'd, to expatiate o'er
The Heliconian pastures, where no plants
Of poison spring, of juice salubrious all,
Which vipers, winding in their verdant track,
Drink, and expel the venom from their tooth,
Dipt in the sweetness of that soil divine.
On him the brave Artontes sinks in death,
Renown'd through wide Bithynia, ne'er again
The clam'rous rites of Cybelé to share;
While echo murmurs through the hollow caves
Of Berecynthian Dindymus.   The strength
Of Alpheus sent him to the shades of night.
Ere from the dead was disengag'd the spear,
Huge Abradates, glorying in his might,
Surpassing all of Cissian race, advanc'd
To grapple; planting firm his foremost step,

The victor's throat he grasp'd. At Nemea's games
The wrestler's chaplet Alpheus had obtain'd.
He summons all his art. Oblique the stroke
Of his swift foot supplants the Persian's heel.
He, falling, clings by Alpheus' neck, and drags
His foe upon him. In the Spartan's back
Enrag'd Barbarians fix their thronging spears.
To Abradates' chest the weapons pass;
They rivet both in death. This Maron sees,
This Polydorus, frowning. Victims, strewn
Before their vengeance, hide their brother's corse.
At length the gen'rous blood of Maron warms
The sword of Hyperanthes. On the spear
Of Polydorus falls the pond'rous ax
Of Sacian Mardus. From the yielding wood
The steely point is sever'd. Undismay'd,
The Spartan stoops to rear the knotted mace
Left by Artuchus; but thy fatal blade,
Abrocomes, that dreadful instant watch'd
To rend his op'ning side. Unconquer'd still,
Swift he discharges on the Sacian's front
A pond'rous blow, which burst the scatter'd brain.
Down his own limbs meantime a torrent flows

Of vital crimson. Smiling, he reflects
On sorrow finish'd, on his Spartan name,
Renew'd in lustre. Sudden to his side
Springs Dithyrambus. Through th' uplifted arm
Of Mindus, pointing a malignant dart
Against the dying Spartan, he impell'd
His spear. The point, with violence unspent,
Urg'd by such vigour, reach'd the Persian's throat
Above his corselet. Polydorus stretch'd
His languid hand to Thespia's friendly youth,
Then bow'd his head in everlasting peace;
While Mindus, wasted by his streaming wound,
Beside him faints and dies. In flow'ring prime
He, lord of Colchis, from a bride was torn,
His tyrant's hasty mandate to obey.
She tow'rd the Euxine sends her plaintive sighs;
She woos in tender piety the winds:
Vain is their favour; they can never breathe
On his returning sail. At once a crowd
Of eager Persians seize the victor's spear.
One of his nervous hands retains it fast,
The other bares his falchion. Wounds and death
He scatters round. Sosarmes feels his arm

Lopt from the shoulder. Zatis leaves entwin'd
His fingers round the long-disputed lance.
On Mardon's reins descends the pond'rous blade,
Which half divides his body. Pheron strides
Across the pointed ash. His weight o'ercomes
The weary'd Thespian, who resigns his hold,
But cleaves th' elate Barbarian to the brain.
Abrocomes darts forward, shakes his steel,
Whose lightning threatens death. The wary Greek
Wards with his sword the well-directed stroke,
Then, closing, throws the Persian. Now what aid
Of mortal force, or interposing heav'n,
Preserves the eastern hero? Lo! the friend
Of Teribazus. Eager to avenge
That lov'd, that lost companion, and defend
A brother's life; beneath the sinewy arm
Outstretch'd, the sword of Hyperanthes pass'd
Through Dithyrambus. All the strings of life
At once relax; nor fame, nor Greece, demand
More from his valour. Prostrate now he lies
In glories, ripen'd on his blooming head.
Him shall the Thespian maidens in their songs
Record, once loveliest of the youthful train,

The gentle, wise, beneficent and brave,
Grace of his lineage, and his country's boast,
Now fall'n. Elysium to his parting soul
Uncloses. So the cedar, which supreme
Among the groves of Libanus hath tow'r'd,
Uprooted, low'rs his graceful top, preferr'd,
For dignity of growth, some royal dome
Or heav'n-devoted fabric to adorn.
Diomedon bursts forward. Round his friend
He heaps destruction. Troops of wailing ghosts
Attend thy shade, fall'n hero! Long prevail'd
His furious arm in vengeance uncontroll'd;
Till four Assyrians on his shelving spear,
Ere from a Cissian's prostrate body freed,
Their pond'rous maces all discharge. It broke.
Still with a shatter'd truncheon he maintains
Unequal fight. Impetuous, through his eye
The well-aim'd fragment penetrates the brain
Of one bold warrior; there the splinter'd wood,
Infix'd, remains. The hero last unsheaths
His falchion broad. A second sees aghast
His entrails open'd. Sever'd from a third,
The head, steel-cas'd, descends. In blood is roll'd

The grizzly beard.   That effort breaks the blade
Short from its hilt.   The Grecian stands disarm'd.
The fourth, Astaspes, proud Chaldæan lord,
Is nigh.   He lifts his iron-plated mace.
This, while a cluster of auxiliar friends
Hang on the Grecian shield, to earth depress'd,
Loads with unerring blows the batter'd helm;
Till on the ground Diomedon extends
His mighty limbs.   So, weaken'd by the force
Of some tremendous engine, which the hand
Of Mars impels, a citadel, high-tow'r'd,
Whence darts, and fire, and ruins, long have aw'd,
Begirding legions, yields at last, and spreads
Its disuniting ramparts on the ground;
Joy fills th' assailants, and the battle's tide
Whelms o'er the wid'ning breach.   The Persian thus
O'er the late-fear'd Diomedon advanc'd
Against the Grecian remnant; when behold
Leonidas!   At once their ardour froze.
He had awhile behind his friends retir'd,
Oppress'd by labour.   Pointless was his spear,
His buckler cleft.   As, overworn by storms,
A vessel steers to some protecting bay;

Then, soon as timely gales inviting curl
The azure floods, to Neptune shews again
Her masts, apparell'd fresh in shrouds and sails,
Which court the vig'rous wind; so Sparta's king,
In strength repair'd, a spear and buckler new
Presents to Asia. From her bleeding ranks
Hydarnes, urg'd by destiny, approach'd.
He, proudly vaunting, left an infant race,
A spouse, lamenting on the distant verge
Of Bactrian Ochus. Victory in vain
He, parting, promis'd. Wanton hope will sport
Round his cold heart no longer. Grecian spoils,
Imagin'd triumphs, pictur'd on his mind,
Fate will erase for ever. Through the targe,
The thick-mail'd corselet, his divided chest
Of bony strength admits the hostile spear.
Leonidas draws back the steely point,
Bent and enfeebled by the forceful blow.
Meantime within his buckler's rim, unseen,
Amphistreus stealing, in th' unguarded flank
His dagger struck. In slow effusion ooz'd
The blood, from Hercules deriv'd; but death
Not yet had reach'd his mark. Th' indignant king

Gripes irresistibly the Persian's throat.
He drags him prostrate. False, corrupt, and base,
Fallacious, fell, pre-eminent was he
Among tyrannic satraps. Phrygia pin'd
Beneath th' oppression of his ruthless sway.
Her soil had once been fruitful; once her towns
Were populous and rich. The direful change,
To naked fields and crumbling roofs, declar'd
Th' accurs'd Amphistreus govern'd. As the spear
Of Tyrian Cadmus rivetted to earth
The pois'nous dragon, whose infectious breath
Had blasted all Bœotia; so the king,
On prone Amphistreus trampling, to the rock
Nails down the tyrant, and the fractur'd staff
Leaves in his panting body. But the blood,
Great hero, dropping from thy wound, revives
The hopes of Persia. Thy unyielding arm
Upholds the conflict still. Against thy shield
The various weapons shiver, and thy feet
With glitt'ring points surround. The Lydian sword,
The Persian dagger, leave their shatter'd hilts;
Bent is the Caspian scymetar; the lance,
The javelin, dart and arrow, all combine

Their fruitless efforts. From Alcides sprung,
Thou stand'st unshaken, like a Thracian hill,
Like Rhodope, or Hæmus; where in vain
The thund'rer plants his livid bolt; in vain
Keen-pointed lightnings pierce th' encrusted snow;
And winter, beating with eternal war,
Shakes from his dreary wings discordant storms,
Chill sleet, and clatt'ring hail. Advancing bold,
His rapid lance Abrocomes in vain
Aims at the forehead of Laconia's chief.
He, not unguarded, rears his active blade
Athwart the dang'rous blow, whose fury wastes
Above his crest in air. Then, swiftly wheel'd,
The pond'rous weapon cleaves the Persian's knee
Sheer through the parted bone. He sidelong falls,
Crush'd on the ground beneath contending feet,
Great Xerxes' brother yields the last remains
Of tortur'd life. Leonidas persists;
Till Agis calls Dieneces, alarms
Demophilus, Megistias: they o'er piles
Of Allarodian and Sasperian dead
Haste to their leader; they before him raise
The brazen bulwark of their massy shields.

The foremost rank of Asia stands and bleeds,
The rest recoil: but Hyperanthes swift
From band to band his various host pervades,
Their drooping hopes rekindles, in the brave
New fortitude excites, the frigid heart
Of fear he warms. Astaspes first obeys,
Vain of his birth, from ancient Belus drawn,
Proud of his wealthy stores, his stately domes,
More proud in recent victory: his might
Had foil'd Plataea's chief. Before the front
He strides impetuous. His triumphant mace
Against the brave Dieneces he bends.
The weighty blow bears down th' opposing shield,
And breaks the Spartan's shoulder. Idle hangs
The weak defence, and loads th' inactive arm,
Depriv'd of ev'ry function. Agis bares
His vengeful blade. At two well-levell'd strokes
Of both his hands, high brandishing the mace,
He mutilates the foe. A Sacian chief
Springs on the victor. Jaxartes' banks
To this brave savage gave his name and birth.
His look erect, his bold deportment, spoke
A gallant spirit, but untam'd by laws,

With dreary wilds familiar, and a race
Of rude Barbarians, horrid as their clime.
From its direction glanc'd the Spartan spear,
Which, upward borne, o'erturn'd his iron cone.
Black o'er his forehead fall the naked locks;
They aggravate his fury; while his foe
Repeats the stroke, and penetrates his chest.
Th' intrepid Sacian through his breast and back
Receives the grinding steel. Along the staff
He writhes his tortur'd body; in his grasp
A barbed arrow from his quiver shakes;
Deep in the streaming throat of Agis hides
The deadly point; then grimly smiles and dies.

From him fate hastens to a nobler prey,
Dieneces.   His undefended frame
The shield abandons, sliding from his arm.
His breast is gor'd by javelins.   On the foe
He hurls them back, extracted from his wounds.
Life, yielding slow to destiny, at length
Forsakes his riven heart; nor less in death
Thermopylæ he graces than before
By martial deeds and conduct.   What can stem

The barb'rous torrent? Agis bleeds. His spear
Lies useless, irrecoverably plung'd
In Jaxartes's body. Low reclines
Dieneces. Leonidas himself,
O'erlabour'd, wounded, with his dinted sword
The rage of war can exercise no more.
One last, one glorious effort age performs.
Demophilus, Megistias, join their might.
They check the tide of conquest; while the spear
Of slain Dieneces to Sparta's chief
The fainting Agis bears. The pointed ash,
In that dire hand for battle rear'd anew,
Blasts ev'ry Persian's valour. Back in heaps
They roll, confounded; by their gen'ral's voice
In vain exhorted longer to endure
The ceaseless waste of that unconquer'd arm.
So, when the giants from Olympus chas'd
Th' inferior gods, themselves in terror shun'd
Th' incessant streams of lightning, where the hand
Of heav'n's great father with eternal might
Sustain'd the dreadful conflict. O'er the field
Awhile Bellona gives the battle rest;
When Thespia's leader and Megistias drop

At either side of Lacedæmon's king.
Beneath the weight of years and labour bend
The hoary warriors. Not a groan molests
Their parting spirits; but in death's calm night
All-silent sinks each venerable head.
Like aged oaks, whose deep-descending roots
Had pierc'd resistless through a craggy slope;
There, during three long centuries, have brav'd
Malignant Eurus, and the boist'rous north;
Till, bare and sapless by corroding time,
Without a blast, their mossy trunks recline
Before their parent hill. Not one remains,
But Agis, near Leonidas, whose hand
The last kind office to his friend performs,
Extracts the Sacian's arrow. Life, releas'd,
Pours forth in crimson floods. O Agis, pale
Thy placid features, rigid are thy limbs;
They lose their graces. Dimm'd, thy eyes reveal
The native goodness of thy heart no more.
Yet other graces spring. The noble corse
Leonidas surveys. A pause he finds,
To mark how lovely are the patriot's wounds,
And see those honours on the breast he lov'd.

But Hyperanthes from the trembling ranks
Of Asia tow'rs, inflexibly resolv'd
The Persian glory to redeem, or fall.
The Spartan, worn by toil, his languid arm
Uplifts once more. He waits the dauntless prince.
The heroes now stand adverse. Each awhile
Restrains his valour. Each, admiring, views
His godlike foe. At length their brandish'd points
Provoke the contest, fated soon to close
The long-continu'd horrors of the day.
Fix'd in amaze and fear, the Asian throng,
Unmov'd and silent, on their bucklers pause.
Thus on the wastes of India, while the earth
Beneath him groans, the elephant is seen,
His huge proboscis writhing, to defy
The strong rhinoceros, whose pond'rous horn
Is newly whetted on a rock. Anon
Each hideous bulk encounters. Earth her groan
Redoubles. Trembling, from their covert gaze
The savage inmates of surrounding woods
In distant terror. By the vary'd art
Of either chief the dubious combat long
Its great event retarded. Now his lance

Far through the hostile shield Laconia's king
Impell'd. Aside the Persian swung his arm.
Beneath it pass'd the weapon, which his targe
Encumber'd. Hopes of conquest and renown
Elate his courage. Sudden he directs
His rapid javelin to the Spartan's throat.
But he his wary buckler upward rais'd,
Which o'er his shoulder turn'd the glancing steel;
For one last effort then his scatter'd strength
Collecting, levell'd with resistless force
The massive orb, and dash'd its brazen verge
Full on the Persian's forehead. Down he sunk,
Without a groan expiring, as o'erwhelm'd
Beneath a marble fragment, from its seat
Heav'd by a whirlwind, sweeping o'er the ridge
Of some aspiring mansion. Gen'rous prince!
What could his valour more? His single might
He match'd with great Leonidas, and fell
Before his native bands. The Spartan king
Now stands alone. In heaps his slaughter'd friends,
All stretch'd around him, lie. The distant foes
Show'r on his head innumerable darts.
From various sluices gush the vital floods;

For one last effort then his scatter'd strength
Collecting, levell'd with resistless force
The massive orb, and dash'd its brazen verge
Full on the Persian's forehead.

Leonidas Book 12

They stain his fainting limbs. Nor yet with pain
His brow is clouded; but those beauteous wounds,
The sacred pledges of his own renown,
And Sparta's safety, in serenest joy
His closing eye contemplates. Fame can twine
No brighter laurels round his glorious head;
His virtue more to labour fate forbids,
And lays him now in honourable rest,
To seal his country's liberty by death.

THE END.

UNIVERSITY OF CALIFORNIA LIBRARY
Los Angeles
This book is DUE on the last date stamped below.

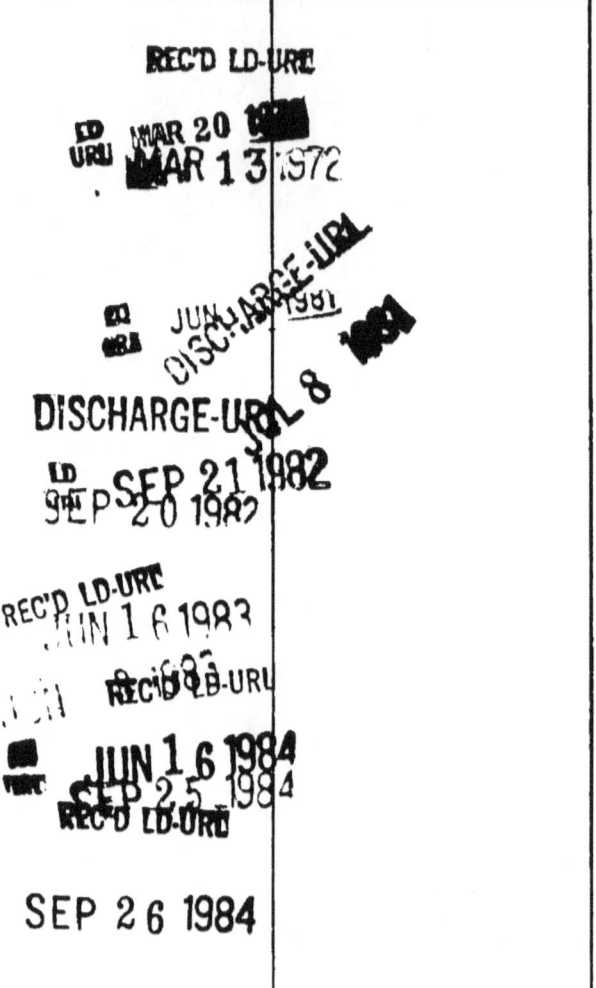

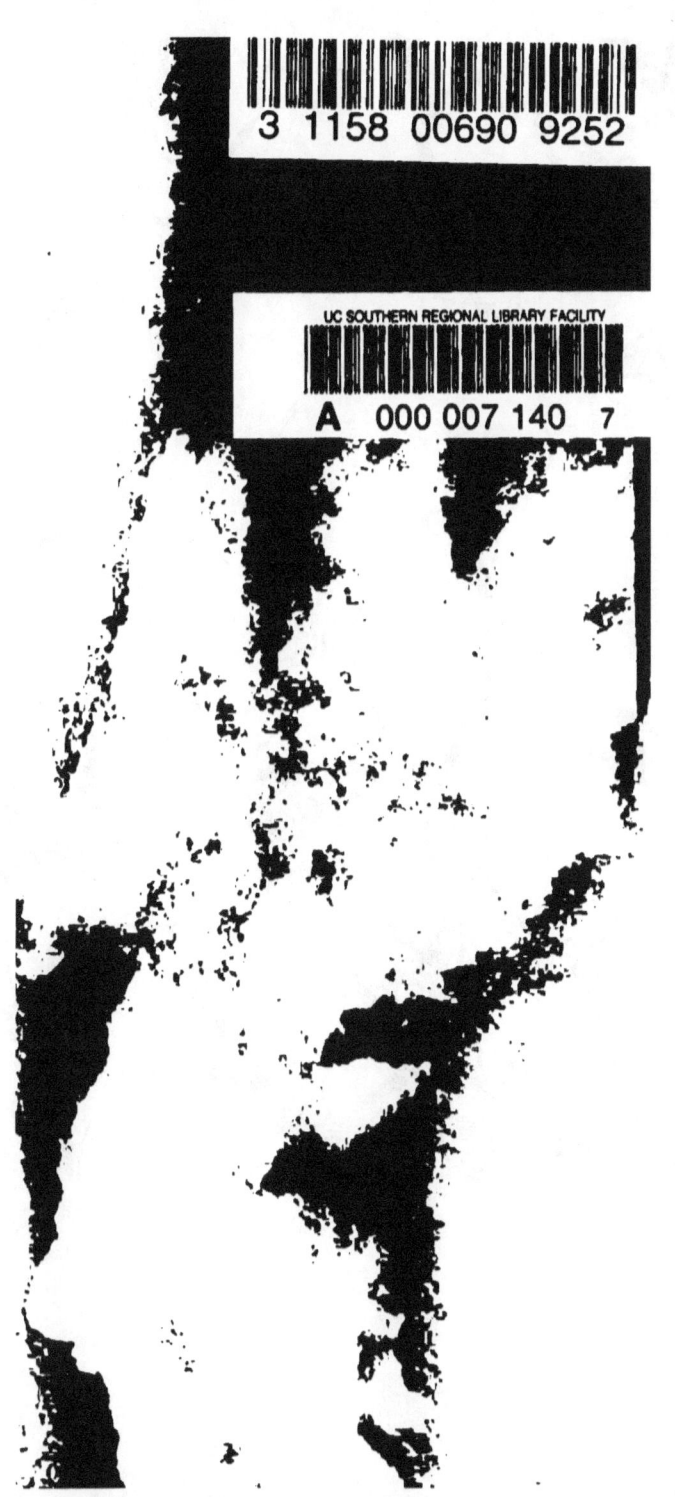

www.ingramcontent.com/pod-product-compliance
Lightning Source LLC
Chambersburg PA
CBHW020903230426
43666CB00008B/1292